Scattered, Smothered,

AND YET COVERED BY THE GRACE OF

God

LISA J. HEYER

WESTBOW
PRESS®
A DIVISION OF THOMAS NELSON
& ZONDERVAN

WestBow Press books may be ordered through booksellers or by contacting:

WestBow Press
A Division of Thomas Nelson & Zondervan
1663 Liberty Drive
Bloomington, IN 47403
www.westbowpress.com
844-714-3454

ISBN: 979-8-3850-1042-4 (sc)
ISBN: 979-8-3850-1043-1 (e)

Library of Congress Control Number: 2023919732

Print information available on the last page.

WestBow Press rev. date: 04/24/2024

I dedicate this book to all the individuals and families that fight the endurance race of life in or with addiction.

There is real hope waiting for you, you only need to be ready to receive it.

It only takes the blood of the Lamb and the faithful word of our testimony to defeat the enemy Satan. They triumphed over him by the blood of the Lamb and by the word of their testimony. They did not love their lives so much as to shrink from death. Revelation 12:11 NIV.

In my words, you lost already, Satan! We have already been saved by the blood of the Lamb, and I am here to tell my testimony!

CONTENTS

PREFACE

Addiction is hard. It is hard on the addict; it is hard on the family and friends, and it is hard on the community.

One of the most important scriptures during these years of addiction was Romans 12:2. Here are a few versions to consider.

Romans 12:1-2

New King James Version

Living Sacrifices to God

I beseech you therefore, brethren, by the mercies of God, that you present your bodies a living sacrifice, holy, acceptable to God, which is your reasonable service. And do not be conformed to this world, but be transformed by the renewing of your mind, that you may prove what is that good and acceptable and perfect will of God.

Romans 12:2 ESV

Do not be conformed to this world, but be transformed by the renewal of your mind, that by testing you may discern what is the will of God, what is good and acceptable and perfect.

Romans 12:1–2 MSG

Place Your Life before God So here's what I want you to do, with God helping you. Take your everyday, ordinary life— your sleeping, eating, going-to-work, and walking-around life and place it before God as an offering. Embracing what God does for you is the best thing you can do for Him. Don't become so well-adjusted to your culture that you fit into it without even thinking. Instead, fix your attention on God. You'll be changed from the inside out. Readily recognize what He wants from you and quickly respond to it. Unlike the culture around you, always dragging you down to its level of immaturity, God brings the best out of you, develops well-formed maturity in you.

The Message is a paraphrase of scripture and the most fitting for this book.

I have been procrastinating writing this book due to the time, emotions, and energy it would take to go back on all these years. It seems when I do not take the time to be obedient in writing, something puts me on my backside, but God led to this scripture as well. 1 Peter 1:13–16, be holy.

1 Peter 1:13-16

Therefore, with minds that are alert and fully sober, set your hope on the grace to be brought to you when Jesus Christ is revealed at his coming. As obedient children do not conform to the evil desires you had when you lived in ignorance. But just as he who called you is holy, so be holy in all you do; for it is written: "Be holy, because I am holy." (1 Peter 1:13–16)

The more I read and studied these scriptures, the more I wanted to know and understand. I often see how God puts something in front of us and places within us a desire to know more. I started searching the commentaries and definitions on this scripture as well.

Commentary on Romans 12
Conformed

It gives us understanding as to what godliness, sobriety, and righteousness are, though somewhat intermixed. Concerning our duty to God, we see what godliness is. It is to surrender ourselves to God and so lay a good foundation. We must first give our own selves unto the Lord. There must be that real holiness which consists of an entire rectitude (morally correct behavior) of heart and life by which we are conformed both to the nature and will of God. Even our bodies must not be made the instruments of sin and uncleanness but set apart for God and put to holy uses as the vessels of the tabernacle were holy, being devoted to God's service.

Renewing of the mind.

Conversion and sanctification are the renewing of the mind, a change not of the substance but of the qualities of the soul. It is the same with making a new heart and a new spirit—new dispositions and inclinations, new sympathies and antipathies, the understanding enlightened, the conscience softened, the thoughts rectified, they will bow to the will of God, and the affections made spiritual and heavenly so that the man is not what he was. Old things have passed away; all things become new.

In 2 Corinthians 3:18, it says that we will be changed into the same image from glory to glory. This transformation is here pressed as a duty, not that we can work such a change ourselves. We could not make a new world, nor make a new heart by any power of our own; it is God's work.

What is glory to glory saying? Create in me a pure heart, O God, and renew a steadfast spirit within me. (Psalm 51:10) But those who hope in the Lord will renew their strength. They will soar on wings like eagles; they will run and not grow weary; they will walk and not be faint. (Isaiah 40:31)

It only takes the blood of the Lamb and the faithful word of our testimony to defeat the enemy Satan. They triumphed over him by the blood of the Lamb and by the word of their testimony. They did not love their lives so much as to shrink from death. Revelation 12:11 NIV.

In my words, you lost already, Satan! We have already been saved by the blood of the Lamb, and I am here to tell my testimony!

And so now it is time to tell of my testimony, the hard long story of my son's addiction and how I was first scattered, then smothered, and at times, it literally felt I was totally covered by the grace of God! And now I have a testimony to write about, a story of hurt and hope and an incredible story of redemption and renewal, all within God's timing. I pray that

God uses me today and every day to glorify Him and that He will make every opportunity available and clear to me that I can share this "Hope" to others. In this He already has!

This is my story, the mother of an addicted son. My son will have his own story to tell when he and God decide the time is right.

I have not used my families' names, because that is not what is important. You can replace "our son" with your son or daughter's name or any other close relationship's name in this situation. The people in your story are yours, but the situation within addiction is always close to the same.

In this, I pray I can be a witness to the love and faithfulness of our God, Lord and Savior, Jesus Christ.

CHAPTER 1

2010

The thief comes only to steal and kill and destroy; I have come that they may have life and have it to the full. —John 10:10 (NIV)

If you knew my story, you'd understand how I know there is power in prayer.

As written in "I Want It All" by Gwen Smith, sifting through emotions like anger, depression, hopelessness, insecurity, and so on is hard stuff! But because we know God, we know all of this as well: His Strength that is accessible in our weakness His Comfort that meets us as we mourn His Mercy that withholds the punishment our depravity readily deserves His Peace that defies our unrest His Joy that kisses the cheeks of our sorrow His Courage that makes our weary hearts brave and casts away fears His Redemption that reworks our brokenness into beauty. His Love that binds us to eternity and delights over us with singing.

All these things that Gwen writes about I see in my journey.

Gwen has written in this book some of the same things God shared with me in my journey: one, that faith is not a feeling, as I wrote in my book Endurance Race of Life and how I learned to "believe God, not just believe in God."

It began in February 2010, a journey of hurt, heartache, and the beginning of destruction and loss. But God...

It begins in February 2010, shortly after our annual Christmas ski trip with our boys where we had a wonderful and very "normal" holiday trip. What none of us knew was that within a couple of months, our lives would change forever. We would be totally broken and scattered into pieces and would never return to what we were or thought we were as a family. We had to find a new normal in a very "unnormal" world. And that would take years.

At fifteen, our youngest son went from what seemed his normal self to having a frenzied look with anger and withdrawal. He changed in what seemed like an instant. That was the reason when we had to check him into a hospital, a behavioral health facility in Chattanooga, Tennessee, we believed he was having some type of mental breakdown. We never dreamed that this condition came over him so quickly from the use of marijuana instead of from some mental condition lurking within him. We were shocked when the doctor told us that he tested positive for marijuana. Our son had been so upset just in the previous year from his older brother drinking beer that we would have never thought he would be drinking, much less using illegal drugs. That is how quickly things can change with teenagers, so be aware of the changes you see in your children. However, not even in hindsight did we see this coming.

But we thought, okay, now we know what has happened, and he will get over this, not use pot anymore now that he sees what it can do to him, and life will go on as planned. Wrong!

I even volunteered that March in 2010 to speak at the women's garden party at our church since I had a story to tell and was ready to share it. I didn't know I was just at the beginning of this story, and there would be almost nine more years of hurt, distress, fear, heartache, and multiple times to experience our son getting close to overdose and death that would follow. Here is a part of what I wanted to share at that women's event; however, God knew it was not time yet. I pray now is the time…

February 2010, everything truly broke loose in our family! From February to June 22, I was going through the worst time ever. I was being scattered; I did not know what to do. I had all the things happen to me from suffering to loss of the child I knew, to tragedy, to heartache all happened at once.

My youngest son, age fifteen, experimented with things he should never have done. He ended up in a behavioral hospital in February with tremendous rage and anger and suicidal threats without us knowing what was going on. It tore our hearts out. Our child seemed fine the previous Christmas on our family ski trip, having a good time… and then January came, and this anger started showing, aggression and anxiety. By February, we had to admit him, and that was when we found out about his substance abuse (pot), and we were shocked. Not our child and especially not our youngest. He is the last we would suspect of doing anything. We thought, well, now we know what is going on, and we can help him. Since that time, it only got worse.

By March he was in another facility in Atlanta because there was use within two weeks of leaving the hospital. The rage and anger started again. He had to be put on homebound to finish school, and we didn't know the use continued. His actions indicated as such, but there was no real proof.

In June, he was arrested for possession and use and, two days later, stopped again with friends that had been using. There is a real drug culture out there that says pot is a natural plant, and God would not have put it there if it were not okay. I reminded my boys that God also has created poison oak and pine trees, and it is natural, but we are not to smoke it!

After fighting for our son for five months with a tremendous amount of heartache, suffering, pain, and loss of twelve pounds (the only complaint I don't have through this), we realized we were working harder to help our son than he was able to help himself, and we knew the time had come to put him in a place of healing, help and to continue his education out of our environment.

Remember again, this is my story, not our son's. He will have his own to tell someday.

That was when I felt as if God was putting me through every Bible story told from Abraham and Isaac, the prodigal son (which unfolded later), to being submissive (which those that know me isn't easy), to letting the man be the head of the household spiritually, to more and more…

Was I to learn all these stories by my own experience? Could I not just read about them in the Bible? I would like to learn one lesson at a time, but that was not how God had chosen to show me. He had allowed me to suffer, struggle, have heartache and loss but, at the same time, used many examples to show me through each one. And when I could not interpret them myself, He had people around me that could.

I am in the middle of my journey. (In hindsight, I was only at the very beginning of my journey. I had eight more years to go. Some things are better left unknown.) The journey is not over, but I know through my faith that I have gained hope, and that gives me the courage to move forward each day. Where there is faith, there is hope, and with hope there is courage to do what is needed.

Having hope will give you courage. Keep your hope alive. I read this on the day that I needed it most. I will share it with you.

"What is at the end of our personal journey is sometimes beyond our wildest imagination. But if we explore the secrets of our heart in light of the promises of scripture, we can discover the clues." John Eldridge, The Sacred Romance.

No eye has seen, no ear has heard, no mind has conceived what God has prepared for those who love Him. (1 Corinthians 2:9)

We cannot outdream God! And yes, I thought I was ready to share this with the women of my church, but God stopped it and made it clear… not now!

As I read and write about this now, I see how clearly, He has used the "not now" with me at the beginning of this journey and the "not now" to giving my testimony to the "not now" in activities that would keep me from giving my testimony!

By September 29, 2010, I was writing My Story 2,
Purpose Driven Life.
My Story 2 September 29, 2010

We all need a purpose in life, whether it be to climb the highest mountain, run a real estate office, or manage a sports team. When we have a purpose, we have something to focus on. When there is no purpose, we flounder. I found that to be the case in my life starting in 2010. In all the previous years of my life, I had a purpose or a goal to reach. I am very goal oriented. I was competing in sports as a young girl, working to complete college, working at goals in a job, and then came the goal of being a wife and a mother. I have never been without a purpose and what was a clear purpose for my life to me, until February 2010.

In 2010, I lost all purpose. I had a fifteen-year-old that was struggling and dealing with anger and drug use, and I totally lost all purpose. I lost my purpose to run a real estate office, I lost my purpose of being a wife, and I couldn't find out how to help my son. So even though I had a purpose to help him, I wasn't successful so, therefore, a failure.

Everything I had ever stood for and worked toward as a goal went down the drain with the helplessness of a struggling child. I was floundering and could not help anywhere.

The sadness started to the point of temporary depression and then the constant crying over my child for fear of what would happen to him and of why we could not help him. I was in total devastation. Each time I thought I had a purpose to work toward to help him, it fell apart.

What was God doing to me, and what did He want me to see?

I know He was trying to show me many lessons in life and to turn to Him for answers, and I tried, but it was still difficult. I offered myself to help any parent that was going through this drug situation because I thought if I have learned anything from this, then I needed to share it with anyone else that was struggling. I thought that could be my purpose. I also offered myself to help at the school if they needed me for information, etc.

I keep looking for my purpose but still not sure where that purpose falls into play. In September 2010, we had to call the police on our son for the second time. He had fallen almost all the way to the bottom. I am not sure how much further he could fall besides in jail or dead.

In 2017–2018, I saw how much further he could fall.

Wow…how I started to see results from all the struggles. My husband stepped up and became the leader in decision-making on placement for our son, became a real prayer leader for him, and took his family leadership to heart. I feel certain that my husband is and will be a better person inside because of this. I have learned to step back, be patient (which is not easy), and wait for someone else to take the lead. Our son, who is the most important person in this situation, is in a safe place with a great godly counselor, Tammy, who loved him from day one. He is in an environment where he should feel good and start to see some success. He needs lots of help, but he is in the right place to get it.

In hindsight again, if he had wanted it and believed he could get it, he could have been better. There is a difference between being clean and being healed. That would take several more years to find out.

I want to give you the backstory if there is one to define. To understand our youngest and who he was will only show you that addiction has no boundaries, not social, economic, geographical limits, or any other limits when it finds its home. It is not selective of race, religion, age; however, the younger it gets you, the harder it is to overcome.

It is important for me to express how anyone—any family, and any one's son or daughter—could be where our son found himself. Addiction does not stay in one arena. It will meet you wherever you are, so beware; the devil comes to kill, steal, and destroy.

When I was pregnant with our youngest, I prayed for a calm child and one that would sleep through the night since the one I had already, which would be eighteen months old when he was born, was very busy, headstrong, and didn't sleep during the night for a couple of years. I was thrilled to have another son, but I just prayed he would not be so overwhelming since I was still dealing with a baby and a hardheaded one at that.

On May 4, our youngest was born. He was beautiful, sweet, calm, and so very loving. While his big brother was running and playing through the house as a busy toddler would do, our youngest would sit and let me rock him, read to him, and love on him. These were not the things I was able to do with his big brother, so I cherished that time.

While one was always busy, the other was content to be with us—go hiking, camping and just be with us as a family. Anyone that knew us then would know that our youngest was also a "Daddy's boy". He loved to be with his dad hiking, camping and, eventually, hiking the AT together for six days. For many years, he was his Dad's shadow, snuggle bug and soulmate, until Satan came to steal, kill, and destroy.

Our youngest was a fun, loving little guy with his own energy and his own style. He did not excel in school, but he gave it his best in the early years. His comments after school every day were that it was boring. If they only had an "outdoor kindergarten" back then, I am certain he would have excelled. He thrived in the outdoors. He would climb the highest mountains, the highest trees and rock formations and then rappel down. We called him our little monkey. He always seemed to be in his element in the great outdoors. He is the second and last child, so he was always our baby. In some cases, he still is in my heart. I am not sure we ever change from our mother's heart no matter what age our children are. We are always Mothers, and they will always be our children.

He grew up under a big brother that could be hard to follow and live with. Our oldest was and still is a strong-minded young man. He is tall, strong, excelled in school, athletics, and socially. Life appeared to be easy for him, at least, from the outside and from his little brother's eyes.

Our youngest is quieter, more reserved, but observed all that was going on around him. He was a more nervous child, and I do not know when or how that started. Was it just who he was? Was it us? Was it others around him? Was it school, bullying, or any other situation that would cause him to feel bad about himself and need something that would take that away or numb it?

We may never know, and he may not ever know how or when it started. He said from the beginning that when he smoked pot for the first time, it was the best day of his life. And that may have been true from his fifteen-year-old perspective. For the first time, he felt calm, accepted, equal to those around him, but that is how the devil gets us and especially those struggling and young. What he thought was the best day of his life was just day one of what would almost take his life and did take eight-plus years of his life and the life of his family.

We all lost over eight years of our lives to heartache, pain, and suffering with his addiction. Addiction is not just for the addicted. It is for all those that are a part of the addict's life, whether in large or small parts.

Satan wants to get us all!

My husband and I married three years after graduating from college. We had our boys while living in Atlanta, and when our boys were two and seven months old, we were offered the opportunity to move back to my hometown to take over the family real estate business.

I had been selling real estate in Atlanta since I graduated college in 1986, and so the opportunity to move back and raise our boys in a safer, less-drug-and-crime-filled community was very appealing. We discussed that we would rather bring our boys up in the small town and know who they went to school with and their families instead of the unknown of Atlanta and their schools.

Let me tell you, addiction will find you where you are and sometimes with some of the ones you would think are "family friends" and "church buddies."

We raised our boys in church. We were there every Sunday and again on Wednesday nights for the children's programs. We were incredibly involved in our church, school, and all the boys' activities. Not only were we involved, but so were my parents and other friends and family.

Our boys were brought up in a loving family, attended church regularly, had a great community, school, and all those blessings and more. So how did we get to where we were in 2010? God only knows, but He would start revealing our false sense of self and our false sense of a relationship with Him that we had and had accepted as good prior.

When our son had to be checked into Parkridge Behavioral Hospital, we found out then was what we thought would be the end of this problem which instead was the beginning of an eight-year nightmare. The doctors noted that he was admitted to Parkridge Valley Hospital for crisis stabilization due to escalating problems with mood management as evident by suicidal ideation, homicidal ideation, and mood lability. He reportedly went into a rage and threatened to kill himself and his father. This was not "our son" and not the one who was "Daddy's little shadow." Where had our son gone and how could we get him back?

Now the backstory on me. This is an important part to see who I was and where I came from, but more importantly, where I would get to.

I was raised in a wonderful loving Christian home. I was the youngest of two. My older brother is five years older and was not thrilled to have me, but that did not stop me from trying to spend all my time following him. I still have the scars on my knees and hand to prove it. I never saw my parents fight, drink, abuse, or use anyone or anything. On the contrary, they loved each other, their family, their community, and those less fortunate than them. My parents were great examples of love, hope, and faith all bundled up in what I could call my family. I was not the easiest to raise for sure, but my mischievous ways never involved drugs. I am not saying I acted great because I didn't do drugs; I am saying that even when I was "bad" and did reckless stuff I shouldn't, I never lost my ability to think clearly and what I did didn't alter my mood, and fortunately, there was no incident that altered my life in any way. I am thankful for that. All things could have turned out much differently, but God!

I have always believed in God. I never remember a time when I did not love God and know that Jesus was the way as stated in John 14:6 (NIV). Jesus answered, "I am the way and the truth and the life. No one comes to the Father except through me." (John 14:6 NIV) I never doubted that, not even once in my life. I was also raised in church which included every Sunday morning, Sunday evening, and on Wednesday nights. And if there was a special event taking place or a revival, we were there. I loved my church and my church family. Many Sundays after church, we would go as a group to play in the park, eat pizza, and grow in our relationships through fellowship. I cannot think of a better way to grow up, and for me, life was comfortable and easy. This is what they now call in church a "community group".

I consider what I had was compared to a chocolate-nut Sunday with a cherry on top; however, I still found the pit! And the pit is where I would stay for the next several years. If you have ever heard that saying that you are only as happy as your sickest child, it is true. I would eventually find some peace through my faith, but I was not happy.

The year it began in 2010 was the hardest year of my life to date. It was the year that I lost my son to addiction for the next eight years. I lost my hope, my purpose in life, and I only really knew and "believed in God"; I didn't know what it was to "believe God" and what He says in His Word.

Our darkest deepest pain can redirect our paths to where God wanted us all along.

What Satan intended for harm; God used for good. You intended to harm me, but God intended it for good to accomplish what is now being done, the saving of many lives. (Genesis 50:20 NIV)

In 2010, we were losing our son to addiction, and there was all the chaos that goes along with addiction.

A dear lady sent me an email that I shared with our son. It was called PUSH. I still have a copy of the email from a sweet lady, Nelda, with this story.

Just Push!

A man was sleeping at night in his cabin when suddenly, his room filled with light, and the Lord told the man He had work for him to do and showed him a large rock in front of his cabin.

The Lord explained that the man was to push against the rock with all his might. So, this the man did day after day. For many years, he toiled from sunup to sundown. His shoulders set squarely against the cold massive surface of the unmoving rock, pushing with all his might.

Each night, the man returned to his cabin sore and worn out, feeling that his whole day had been spent in vain.

Since the man was showing discouragement, the Adversary (Satan) decided to enter the picture by placing thoughts into the weary mind. You have been pushing against that rock for a long time, and it hasn't moved. Thus, it gave the man the impression that the task was impossible, and that he was a failure…and to do the minimum effort.

That was what he planned to do but decided to make it a matter of prayer and take his troubled thoughts to the Lord.

"Lord," he said, "I have labored long and hard in your service, putting all my strength to do that which you have asked. Yet after all this time, I have not even budged that rock by half a millimeter. What is wrong? Why am I failing?"

The Lord compassionately explained to the man that he never once expected the man to push with all his strength upon the rock and move it. The man thought he had failed the Lord. The Lord showed him that certainly wasn't the case. He pointed out the man's arms and how strong and muscled they now were, his back sinewy and brown, and how his hands were callused from constant pressure, and how the man's legs had become massive and hard. Through opposition, the man had grown so much, and his abilities now surpass that what he used to have. The Lord reminded him that he may have not moved the rock, but the Lord called him to be obedient and to push and to exercise his faith and trust in the Lord's wisdom. This the man had done. The Lord then moved the rock.

At times, when we hear a word from God, we tend to use our own intellect to decipher what He wants when what God wants is just a simple obedience and faith in Him. By all means, exercise the faith that moves mountains but know that it is still God who moves mountains.

When everything seems to go wrong just PUSH! When the job gets you down just PUSH! When people don't react the way you think they should…just PUSH! When your money is gone, and the bills are due…just PUSH! When people just don't understand you…just PUSH!

P + U + S + H = Pray + Until + Something + Happens Just push!

Nelda blessed us in many ways from the very beginning of this journey with our son. She sent me an email telling me God must have big plans for him to be allowing all this in his life. This story, her prayers, love, and encouragement helped me so much over the years. It gave me hope when what all I could see was hopelessness. I hope that I can do the same for others. Just a little hope can go a long way in this battle.

As a parent in this situation, you just need a little hope to get you through the next day or sometimes the next minute. Also, as a parent, you will grasp any idea or opportunity that might help just because it worked for someone else.

One theory came from a facility we had considered called Capstone Treatment Center. Our son did not go there, but their residents received a puppy on arrival. They use canine therapy in their program, and we discussed with them how they used the pup to add in the healing of addiction. You can find all their information on their website, https://www.capstonetreatmentcenter.com, but for us, we did what many desperate parents would do. We bought our son a dog, more specifically, a chocolate Lab that he named Stihl. I do not recommend doing this unless you are ready to raise a puppy. It did not change our son, but we were blessed to have Stihl for almost 13 years, and he was the sweetest, most loving dog we have ever had. 2010-2023

We were not trained to use canine therapy, and what our son needed would not be coming from us. He needed help we could not provide, but that did not stop us from trying everything. So, the dog thing did not work. Taking his best friend on a trip with him thinking the friend was a good influence did not work. The two would sneak off and get high together. The medications, the counseling, the fighting…none of it worked. Our son would not stay at Capstone as we had hoped. He was literally losing it and his dad would not leave him there. I do not know if it would have made a difference if we had walked away and left him there, but that was not what we did. We brought him home without a plan but with his dog, Stihl.

Our son was at a terrible place in his life, and we didn't' have a clue what to do. And if you have this situation, you know that most of the time, the addict is as confused as you are and wants to blame everything that is happening to them on you.

We were blamed for **Everything**! We checked him into a program in Alabama, but that lasted thirty days, and he said he learned more about hard drugs there than he knew prior to going. I do not doubt that to be true. I believe every facility and program he attended only gave him more knowledge of drugs. It just depended on how he used that knowledge for good or bad. And he used it for bad. He became obsessed with the drug culture instead of being deterred from it.

Where I was in 2010 is shown by the "Impact Letter" I wrote to my son. Impact Letter November 14, 2010. We were asked to write one to our son while he was getting help in a facility.

This was my impact letter written out of pure honesty of emotions but with much love. It was not intended to hurt our son but to make him truly aware of the effects of his drug life on those around him that love him.

The impact of our son's drug use on me and my family…

1. His drug use took away my son. He was not himself anymore. He was angry, aggressive, and a stranger to me. I mourned the loss of my son.

2. His drug use cost me the loss of fun times I should have had with my son. It stole the last one to two years of my life with him and with others. (It eventually stole eight-plus years.)

3. His drug use caused physical and emotional stress. I was physically sick. I could not eat, sleep, or function due to excessive worry for him. Emotionally, I became so depressed because I hurt and feared for my child. My life felt as if I had buried my youngest son and put a stranger in his place. Each time we faced an arrest, police involvement, hospitalization, I would think this is it, now it is over, and he has learned his lesson. So, I faced repeated disappointments.

4. His drug use made me hurt and angry and left me with many questions. When our son would threaten to kill us, threaten suicide, tell us he hated us, break cabinets, run away, curse us, tell us we were dead to him, I would be so hurt. How could someone I have loved so much and done all I could for act that way? Then the anger would come. How can he do this to us when all we have ever done is to love him, provide abundantly for him, and risk everything for him? Why would anyone choose a drug over the love of family? How could someone pick personal pleasure over a loving family? I would do anything for the people I love, including sacrificing my life or my life's desires if necessary.

5. His drug use could have cost me my marriage and my relationship with our older son.

I had to get counseling to know how to handle the stresses of an addicted child and not let it destroy other relationships that are important to me. My worry and stress affected my job, my relationships, and my health. It is amazing that just one person's choices in life have caused my life and those around us to crumble. I am determined not to let my family fall apart, and my husband feels the same way, or we would not have survived the devastation we have both felt.

6. His drug use has caused me to be angry because of the effects it had on our other son. We missed many events and basketball games in February and March. We could not be there for him many times because we were dealing with our addicted son's problems.

    Our oldest son had to face his brother's drug use and the heartache at only seventeen. We hurt for him because he lost his brother and did not know how to explain his behavior or situation. How do you tell your friends your brother has been arrested and is a drug addict?

7. His drug use caused tremendous worry for my parents, his Mimi and Pop. They hurt so much for him and cried for him and loved him unconditionally without any judgment, and he would not speak to them, see them, or write to them. I have hurt so much for them. It was my parents, he was hurting. He was hurting all the people that I have loved including himself.

8. His drug use caused loss of trust. I do not know how long it will take to trust him again. It is so hard to know someone will lie to you and continuously manipulate you for their own benefit. Trust is so important to me, and I have lost it completely.

9. His drug use took away a year of happiness from me. He hurt me, all our family, and others close to him. My world was shattered. We gave and were willing to do everything to help him, and he chose drugs over the love and happiness of his family. (Actually, it took eight-plus years of happiness from me)

10. His drug use caused resentment. I resent him for blaming us. What did we have to gain by his choice to use drugs? He chose to do wrong but wants to blame us for his behavior—we make him angry; we make him want to use, we make his life miserable, we are horrible parents… We taught him better than that. We educated him on not using drugs…then he blames us for messing up his life.

11. His drug use has given us more responsibility. He wanted a chocolate Lab puppy to focus on and train. We spent lots of money on the puppy he wanted, and now we have Stihl to raise. We are raising and taking care of his dog. We must come home every day for lunch to take him out. We must find boarding when we need to travel. We love him, but he was our son's responsibility, but our mistake, thinking it would work.

12. His drug use cost us financially. We had dreams and plans of what we would do now and in the future. The expense of his hospitalization, school, medical treatment has taken those plans away. We will not take the trips we had planned. We will have to be more careful with our money for college educations, we will work longer, etc.

When our son chose drugs, we lost our hearts, our savings account, our joy, our family, our emotions, both our son's high school years, our health, but with all this, it didn't steal our faith. Satan came to steal, kill, and destroy, but God came that we may have life, and have it to the full.

It only made my faith grow!

Because I have tremendous faith in God and know through Him "all things are possible," I do believe that if our son desired to open his heart to God and ask Him to fill him with a complete recovery and replace the desires of his heart with good, that all that had been lost and hurt would be removed. Our relationship could have been better than ever. Our love for each other would have strengthened beyond what we could imagine.

I truly understand God's unconditional love He has for each of us more than ever now because I have that for my children. No matter all the hurt and pain I have been through in my son's addiction, it has not lessened my love for our son. I love him as much as I did the day he was born. I love him more than my own life. So, I pray that he will be free of his addiction, but I will always love him.

With all this being written, yes, I have felt: Anger, fear, depression, insecurities, financial strain, stress, distrust, sadness, resentment, sickness, hurt, worry and much more…but I love our son and know I also have felt forgiveness. I forgive him now because he did not have the tools needed to fight addiction. It was the addiction that was hurting us, and in my heart, I knew that was not our son.

But what happens from here is his responsibility because he has been offered opportunities and tools where he is staying now including a loving and caring counselor, Tammy.

My faith and love in our son gives me the courage to keep going.

To our son, you are a strong-willed young man. Make your will be what offers you the best in life for yourself and those around you. I love you with all my heart and cannot wait to have my son back.

Love, Mom

I would get him back and with a renewed heart but not until 2018, eight years later.

A special blessing to me and my family—my parents that never gave up, put up with so much, and my dad for saving my son's life by teaching him all he could. My dad gave our son a life to build a foundation from.

What a blessing to have a heavenly Father and earthly father that has so much love for us, that our heavenly Father would give His own Son for us, and both would give their own life for any one of us!

We are blessed and loved!

Where 2010 began and where it ended were on total ends of the spectrum. In February 2010, I thought that our son had fallen to the bottom into drug use but that with some changes, he would and could be okay. I was overwhelmed by the depth of which he fell and that he was nowhere near getting better but, instead, getting worse. Also, what I found out about myself during this year versus what I would do and become over the next few years, would not only transpire, but would show me where my faith was at the time, which was in the church activities and not in the heart of God. What I needed the most, my church could not give me. Only when I withdrew from the "norm" of church activities out of desperation did I find who I needed, far greater than anything I knew or activity I had done.

I fell into the arms of God searching for help, needing to be held and led in a direction that was foreign to me. I needed to surrender to the One that held the key. That did not happen overnight. It did not even happen in the first few years, but it did happen. And when it did, my world changed, and so did others around me!

CHAPTER 2

YEAR 2011

Satan, the Father of Lies. What Does Satan Tell Us?

He was a murderer from the beginning, not holding to the truth, for there is no truth in him. When he lies, he speaks his native language, for he is a liar and the father of lies. —John 8:44

So, when I was still searching for my purpose and how to help our son and our family's survival, on May 11, 2011, I wrote what I called My Story 3, "What Do You Have for My Heart?"

My Story 3.

May 11, 2011. It all began when I felt the need to find what God had in store for me. I needed to find a place away from home to "eat, pray, and love." I chose the beach because I find peace there! This time, I felt God there; that is real peace! I was trying to find my calling in all my life's trials and tribulations. I knew God had a plan for me, and I just had to find how to open my heart and let Him show me.

I arrived at the beach with a dear friend on Monday evening, May 2, 2011. On Tuesday, we spent the day in the condo, me working on paperwork, quotes, writings from the past one and a half years. I felt the need to organize my thoughts and papers. It was the first day that I could ever remember being at the beach on a beautiful day and being very content to work on paper and work inside!

I got a lot done, but I was still trying to see where God was leading me.

That Wednesday morning when I got up, I decided to start my devotional reading, etc.

There it was…the beginning for me and for my journey. What hit home was written in John Eldridge's book Waking the Dead:

The Glory of a Heart Fully Alive, on page 216.

"Let me ask again… What does your heart need? A simple starting place would be to ask God: "What do you have for my heart?" You will be stunned by what he guides you into." John Eldridge

I already knew before traveling to Florida that my mission was about the heart and my heart, but I did not know where that was to lead. And that is where my walk began! I will call it my spirit walk!

I turned on my iPod, which people used in 2011, to WOW Hits 2010 and put it on shuffle. And then He spoke to me through those songs.

As I walked down the beach toward the pier, the words of God came to me through the song "City on Our Knees" by TobyMac. He told me to start at home, our little city of LaFayette. God said to speak to the people about the heart of our people and the heart of our town. Our children and families are suffering. We are at war, and we need to come together and get on our knees.

I grew up in a traditional church, FBC of LaFayette, but spent more time on Sundays getting pinched in church and getting spanked after church for talking by my mom. I was always there, and I have always believed, but I was not really seeking God until my world fell apart. Isn't that what most of us do? Only seek God when we are in real need.

I did not even know how to really seek God. I played, not on purpose, the traditional Christian role. Raise a family with good values, go to church on Wednesdays and Sundays, and be a good person. What did that get me…a scattered and smothered broken heart!

But God has a plan for me just like He does for everyone who believes and asks Him "What do you have for my heart?"

He said to me on that day, you can talk to your city, you can get them to come together and get them on their knees. You can influence the superintendent of the schools, the administrators, the leaders to see what is really happening, to remove the scales from their eyes and get their heads out of the sand and stand up for our children and our communities.

I recall when I called the high school to talk to them about the drug use within the school and the students passing around drugs during class that the assistant principal I spoke to said "We don't have a drug problem" which was either denial with full scales over their eyes, or a total lie because I was hearing it from my son and seeing the effects of it on him and many others.

Now as time has passed, and we are now 10+ years later, the opioid epidemic has become clear and those people who were in denial or lying have seen it clearly. It is no longer hidden from anyone.

This is what I was hearing from God.

You can start by speaking to churches in the area. Start one by one and then plan a city coming together, event. This would become what was called Walker County Cities on Our Knees.

I know those that know me well, dread when I say "I have an idea" because that usually means something that needs to be moved, an event planned, or it could mean just any wild idea I have come up with that will involve their efforts. This time God has an idea, and I am just helping Him orchestrate it!

Through me, I hoped and prayed that His will is done!

My checklist included some of the following:

1. We must recognize our town has a drug problem (adults and teens).

2. We must acknowledge we can do something about it.

3. We must come together for our children and families.

4. We must provide support and comfort for those families suffering.

5. We must have a plan but be willing to change as needed.

6. We must be a "City on Our Knees." Praying for our people as it says in 2 Chronicles 7:14

If My people, who are called by My name, will humble themselves and pray, and seek My face and turn from their wicked ways, then I will hear from heaven, and will forgive their sin and will heal their land.

Who needs to attend?

Do we need counselors, pastors, city officials, addicts, NA groups, AA groups, teenage program groups? What resources?

This will be a community-wide planned event.

Leave time to speak about suggestions and resources they may have available. Someone will be there to take notes!

Get contact information and prayer request for any follow up support.

Acknowledgments: God first, My family for the "scattered mess in the hallway" that led me to seek God.

Whenever God closes one door, He always opens another, even though sometimes it is a scattered mess in the hallway!

There was a purpose for me, and God was beginning to show me.

Scriptures that played a part:

Above all else, guard your heart, for it is the wellspring of life. Proverbs 4:23 This is also versed "for it determines the course of your life."

Praise the Lord, O my soul. Psalm 104. This is an appreciation of God through His creation.

Where your treasure is, there your heart will be also.

Matthew 6:21

And this is for me and my family...

For I know the plans I have for you, declares the Lord, plans to prosper you, and not harm you, plans to give you hope and a future. Then you will call upon me and come and pray to me, and I will listen to you. You will seek me and find me when you seek me with all your heart. Jeremiah 29:11–13

There is a saying that goes:

Happiness keeps you sweet, Trials keep you strong, Sorrows keep you human, Failures keep you humble, Success keeps you glowing But only God keeps you going!

The Father of Lies stopped me writing for a few weeks. He also kept me trapped. He can convince us of anything that we allow him to speak to us. Don't listen to his lies.

It has been extremely hard reliving the past years where all the hurt and heartache began. I started feeling inadequate to write, speak, share... I started feeling like "Why do I think I have anything to share?" "Why would God use me?" "Why me when I am not that knowledgeable in scriptures, writing, or speaking?"

And then after a few weeks of internally fighting inside with "write or not write," I remembered God does not use the equipped; He equips those He chooses to use. And so many times, He uses those that are the least able, and that is where we can glorify Him. Not only do we know we are not able, but others know we aren't able either. And because we are not able, God is the only obvious answer to our why and how!

How many times have you heard or felt like it is **Impossible** or there is **No Hope** for me or for them? Do not believe that lie. Anything is possible with Christ who strengthens us. That is **Truth**! As Jesus says, "my grace is sufficient for you, for my strength is made perfect in your weakness.

I can do all things through Christ who strengthens me. Philippians 4:13 NKJV

So, I start again, this time remembering Satan is the Father of Lies, and as it is said in the Scriptures: They triumphed over him by the blood of the Lamb and by the word of their testimony; they did not love their lives so much as to shrink from death. Revelation 12:11

May the God of peace, who through the blood of the eternal covenant brought back from the dead our Lord Jesus, that great Shepherd of the sheep, equip you with everything good for doing his will, and may he work in us what is pleasing to him, through Jesus Christ, to whom be glory for ever and ever. Hebrews 13:20–21.

Since God's truth triumphed over Satan by the blood of the Lamb, and has already been completed, and the word of our testimony is how we triumph over Satan, the Father of Lies, then it is my turn to tell my story, my testimony of my faith.

I do not have to worry if I can because He says He will equip me for everything good for doing His will. If He has placed this on my heart, all I must do is be obedient to His calling.

2011 was a horrendous year, but there were blessings in it still.

We were still learning about our son, how to continue to get him in a better place physically, spiritually, and mentally, but it felt like we were one step forward and ten steps back on most days. He was in a facility where he was getting counseling, working on his GED, and staying away from our area, but he also had friends that wanted to keep him where he was in his use of drugs. This was a hard time to be a parent versus a friend. We wanted him to grow healthy, but the friends wanted him to continue with his use and to do it with them. We were the "insane ones," the parents that would not accept this behavior unlike some of the other parents of these kids. The battle was real. We wanted our son to get clean, healthy, and be successful in life; however, others just wanted their kids to love them and, therefore, Let Anything Go! Not only would they not punish their children, but they would also bail them out of trouble. This happened many times in 2011 and the years to follow.

We fought this battle continuously and would never give into what society said was okay and what others were allowing their kids to get away with. I can say now that it was worth the battle. Our son did not like us for many years, but he knew we loved him and were fighting for him. He came out of the other side of this battle a better person. Some of these other kids are still fighting their battles, in prison or dead from their parents' acceptance of their behavior.

Parents, please do not let your desire for your children's love become more important to you than the role you play as a parent. During times like these, they do not need a friend; they need a parent that has their best at heart. If I had made our relationship more about our son loving me during these years, he would probably be dead or in prison, which would have been more hurtful and harmful than what we had to endure during those years.

Love is not always saying Yes! Most times during situations like these, real love is saying No! Your child may not like you, and probably will not, but later, they know you did all you could to prevent their destruction, whether they failed or succeeded in their addiction.

In this year, I felt like I could not breathe, move, work, or do anything else. I felt frozen in a state of hurt and sadness. My husband and I had to make an extra effort to step out of the situation and find a day or two of peace somehow and somewhere, but not at our home. When you are stuck in such a stressful event, it is so important to find your calm and peaceful self, if only for a day. Step out of your normal surroundings, pray, breathe, and feel some freedom that you cannot feel when you are right in the middle of it. And when you step out of the battle, sometimes new ideas will come. Allow yourself to refocus and allow rest for your heart and mind.

Even though this year was one of the worst because we had to send our son off to get him out of our environment for his well-being, we still didn't know what we were really dealing with. He hated us and wanted at times to be "emancipated" from us. We had terrible phone conversations with him, but he did get his GED during this time. He was safe, and he was getting some tools that he could use then and later in this journey, even if he didn't recognize it at the time.

In May of 2011, our son graduated from Eckerd and graduated with his GED diploma. The next day, our other son graduated from high school as well.

Our youngest son would be home now, and it was just the continuation of addiction and the behaviors that go along with it. It would continue from his first day back home. He was depressed and totally down on himself. He wanted me to hear this song that he said, "fits him."

What Now? By Rihanna

I been ignoring this big lump in my throat
I shouldn't be crying, tears were for the weak
The days I'm stronger, know what, so I say
That's something missing
Whatever it is, It feels like it's laughing at me through the glass of a two-sided mirror
Whatever it is, It's just sitting there laughing at me
And I just wanna scream
What now? I just can't figure it out
What now? I guess I'll just wait it out

What now? Oh, oh, oh, oh, what now? …
…What now? Somebody tell me
What now?
I don't know where to go
I don't know what to feel
I don't know how to cry
I don't know how or why

Our son was so deep into addiction by this first year. He was lost. At this point, I felt as if I had been told that our son has cancer, and nobody knew if he would live or die or how long he had. It felt like a terminal disease. Addiction was his "cancer", and a facility was his "chemo." And all we could do as parents was pray, pay for his treatment, and love him through it.

My world was falling apart, and my child was dying before my very eyes. And then there was our other son. He was lost, struggling with his own issues, and we had to ask him to leave as well. He was using pot and wanted us to understand why that should be okay. Nothing was okay at that point.

And that was when he decided to head off to college in Colorado and take our addicted son with him. He said it would help his brother by being away from home, and he would work and go to school, while his brother found a job doing something.

All I can say about that adventure was they were gone for eight weeks, and we had some peace and they had unhealthy fun.

It was an unhealthy summer vacation for them in Colorado that year with no lessons learned from them except they weren't ready for freedom and responsibilities.

They came back days before our oldest was to start college, messed up and no better than when they left. However, he did start college locally to get headed in the right direction. Our other son would still be lost in the stronghold of addiction.

I had to keep reminding myself, let go and let God!

I would repeatedly need this reminder because letting go of your child, no matter what age, is a difficult and unnatural thing to do, especially if you are the mother.

About this time, my husband and I started seeing the numbers 638 everywhere. At first, it was just me, and I was telling him about it, and then he began to see it. It would be on our clocks right when we looked, on our car radio, and on signs. It seemed to be everywhere. That was when I realized there was more to this than coincidence. God was trying to get me to see something. What was it?

It was a sign from God that I needed to figure out, but what was it and how could I find out? I started looking up every verse in the Bible that had a 6:38 in it. There were only seven (the perfect number, complete) places in Scripture that there was a 6:38, and I pinpointed John 6:38 as the verse that I was supposed to see.

For I have come down from heaven not to do my will but to do the will of him who sent me. John 6:38 NIV

Later, I would conclude that it was Luke 6:38. I will get into that more in Chapter 6, year 2016.

Give, and it will be given to you. A good measure, pressed down, shaken together, and running over, will be poured into your lap. For with the measure you use, it will be measured to you. Luke 6:38 NIV

In writing in 2019, I believe both verses, along with the others, are what I was to see—in His timing, not immediately, and not all at once.

In Luke 6:38, I needed to give, and I could never outgive God, and in John 6:38, to follow the example of doing the will of God, not my will. But in reviewing the seven different verses, it could have also been Judges 6:38 where Gideon asked for a sign, and God gave him the sign.

And that is what happened. Gideon rose early the next day; he squeezed the fleece and wrung out the dew—a bowlful of water. Judges 6:38 NIV

And could it also include 1 Kings 6:38? I thought no at the time, but then in hindsight, I see it took seven years to get me where I needed to be in our son's addiction. He would struggle in his addiction for eight years, and then it was finished. God spent seven years building it (our son and me). So, in what I learned in this last year, this verse could have also been a sign, one that I would not recognize in 2011, but one I could see at the end of 2019.

In the eleventh year in the month of Bul, the eighth month, the temple was finished in all its details according to its specifications. He had spent seven years building it. 1 Kings 6:38 NIV

And it could also be for a time such as this when our son repented, was saved, and baptized in the Cullasaja River in Franklin, North Carolina.

When they sin against you—for there is no one who does not sin—and you become angry with them and give them over to the enemy, who takes them captive to a land far away or near; and if they have a change of heart in the land where they are held captive, and repent and plead with you in the land of their captivity and say, "We have sinned, we have done wrong and acted wickedly"; and if they turn back to you with all their heart and soul in the land of their captivity where they were taken, and pray toward the land you gave their ancestors, toward the city you have chosen and toward the temple I have built for your Name; then from heaven, your dwelling place, hear their prayer and their pleas, and uphold their cause. And forgive your people, who have sinned against you. 2 Chronicles 6:36–39 NIV

The other two 6:38 verses may not yet seem to fit, but I know God and His timing isn't always our timing, and therefore, there may be a time that all the 6:38 verses have a place in my story.

1 Chronicles 6:38

The son of Izhar, the son of Kohath, the son of Levi, the son of Israel. 1 Chronicles 6:38 NIV

Mark 6:38

"How many loaves do you have?" he asked. "Go and see." When they found out, they said, "Five— and two fish." Mark 6:38 NIV

In August 2011, I read this devotional, The Secret Is Surrender.

Don't you know that when you offer yourselves to someone as obedient slaves, you are slaves of the one you obey—whether you are slaves to sin, which leads to death, or to obedience, which leads to righteousness? Romans 6:16 NIV

In the devotional it says, "Instead of filling your mind with resentments, abusing your body by sinful diversion, and damaging your soul by willfulness, humbly give all over to God. Your conflicts will diminish, and your inner tensions will often vanish. Then your life will begin to count for something.

It will begin to yield, to produce, to bear fruit. You will have the feeling of belonging to life. Boredom will melt away, and you will become vibrant with hope and expectation. Because you are meekly yielded, you will begin to "inherit the earth" of good things which God holds in store for those who trust Him with their all."

This devotional speaks as much volume today as it did in 2011.

This is something we need to always keep in the forefront.

CHAPTER 3

YEAR 2012

Be joyful in hope, patient in affliction, faithful in prayer.
Romans 12:12 (NIV)

About this time, I began realizing that we were not done and nowhere close to being in a better place. My hope was dwindling, and my patience with all the affliction was not what it should or had been. I tried with all I had to be faithful in prayer and ask others to also be in prayer. This was not a situation that I could fix with a mom's heart as much as I wanted to.

My Story 4, written on August 22, 2012. I guess God had me writing these stories so that someday, I could go back and see the parts I had to walk through, see how He would use me, and see what I would need to share someday to help others.

What Satan meant for bad, God would use for good.

I had hoped that My Story 3 would be the end of something good, but no, the story was far from over. I last wrote My Story 3 in May 2011. After that, I not only had my youngest son to deal with, but I was dealing with our oldest son too.

How could I handle my two boys at the same time?

We had a terrible summer, until our sons moved to Colorado together. We had peace at home, and I think "out of sight, out of mind" was the only reason why. We really hoped they would learn to live and survive and want better than the choices they had made. Once again, wrong! They were to bound to what they were into. I told them," Unless you change, you will find yourself wherever you are! Changing towns, states, etc. doesn't do the job."

Basically, May through December 2011 were once again a scattered mess in our household and hearts, but then we finally decided to put in place for 2012 what we had been told and read…let go and let God.

January 2012 became that for us. We had been trying in 2011 to do that, but we would let go and then take it back. We could not control them, so we had to turn them over to God.

Our youngest would be eighteen in May, and oldest was nineteen. So, for us, that was our time to say you are responsible for yourself. You may choose this life, but you will also support yourself in it.

In March, the boys moved out, paid for everything, lived together (the odd couple for those that remember that show and for those that know them), and learned what it would be to work and be responsible.

Many events and situations happened during that time, but when we let go and let God, He did so much more for them than we ever could. I can say in letting go and not feeling I am responsible for anyone's actions but mine, is freeing. I can love them unconditionally, but I do not have to support their actions or bail them out.

As of August 2012, we had seen both boys grow so much. They moved back into our home at the end of July. Our oldest started following his choice of education and football and left for Reinhardt University on August 19, 2012, to play football and work on his education. Our youngest is planning to move to Colorado at the end of the month and work in construction, where he had gained so much knowledge and ability in, thanks to the unconditional love and training from my dad.

Both are starting their adult paths in a healthier way, and I prayed that would continue, but I know all I can do about it is pray for them. The rest is between them and God.

This time, when we said goodbye, it was with such peace and a loving relationship. Our relationships have begun growing strong again.

I have learned more about our heavenly Father's grace and unconditional love and because of God's unconditional love I was able to have the same grace and unconditional love with my earthly children.

I have always been given unconditional love by my parents and my heavenly Father, and it allowed me to desire the same through this process. I see now that we do not experience one testimony but a reoccurrence of testimonies or a continuation of testimonies, each having a special place for us to share.

I do not think this will be the last time I write my testimony, but I do know in these last two and a half years of this process, I have grown so much. The trials and tribulations have been enormous, but with tremendous blessings as well. (And no, it would not stop there but would get much worse before it would get better. This was only 2012, and unknown to me, there would be six to seven more hard years).

The verses to remember in times like these are.

James 1:2–6.

Consider it pure joy, my brothers, and sisters, whenever you face trials of many kinds, because you know that the testing of your faith produces perseverance. Let perseverance finish its work so that you may be mature and complete, not lacking anything. If any of you lacks wisdom, you should ask God, who gives generously to all without finding fault, and it will be given to you. But when you ask, you must believe and not doubt, because the one who doubts is like a wave of the sea, blown and tossed by the wind. James 1:2–6

I did not feel joy at all, but the testing of my faith did produce perseverance, and I did become much more mature and complete in my faith and the real knowledge of who God is. And as a doctor in the hospital emergency room in the psychiatric ward told me on one of the first trips we had to make with our son, "Pray with expectations for him." He meant not only to pray for our son, but pray believing in what we could not see at the moment. Faith is believing in what we can't see, and I couldn't see how our son was going to survive this, but faith isn't seeing or a feeling; it is believing God's got this and out of my hands.

This was over seven years ago when I was writing My Story 4, and I still remember being scared, heartbroken, and yet comforted by these true reminders of God's faithfulness.

God gave this doctor the desire to share with me the message of faith that I needed at that moment. I am not sure where I saw this promise, but I took the time in 2012 to print it and put it in my journal. It still resonates with me because I have seen this in our journey as we went from being the parent and loved by my son to being hated while I searched, lectured, and hunted him down literally only to save his life from himself.

It was not the time to be his friend; it was time to be his mother searching for hope, praying for patience, and continuously being faithful in prayer.

Our promise to our children—as long as I live—I am your parent first, your friend second. I will stalk you, lecture you, drive you insane, be your worst nightmare, and hunt you down like a bloodhound when needed because I Love You! When you understand that, I will know you are a responsible adult.

You will never find someone who loves, prays, cares, and worries about you more than I do! If you do not hate me once in your life, I am not doing my job properly.

Concentrate on this sentence… To get something you never had, you must do something you never did. When God takes something from your grasp, He is not punishing you but merely opening your hands to receive something better.

The will of God will never take you where the grace of God will not protect you.

So, remember just twenty-seven words…

God our Father, walk through my house and take away all my worries and illnesses and please watch over and heal my family in Jesus's name. Amen.

What I thought our son needed to see, hear, and believe was what I discovered was so true in my life. It would take several years from this point to see how I could and would receive something better, but I did, and the will of God was always connected to the grace of God, and the freedom and blessings that came through this journey is unbelievable.

I had bondages, hurts, and hang-ups I did not even know I had, but most importantly, I had a false sense of faith in my relationship with God. Throughout these trials, more of this false sense of faith was exposed to me.

Hope deferred makes the heart sick, but a longing fulfilled is a tree of life. (Proverbs 15:48 NIV)

There is so much truth in this. Not only did my deferred hope make my heart sick, it also physically took its toll on me. I was physically, spiritually, and mentally a wreck. I was sick from the inside out. I wanted what was normal for my family and especially my children, but we were nowhere near normal to me.

Nothing I had thought, planned, and expected looked like a son battling the full force of addiction and what it would do to him and to our family. I had to hope for better, but it is so hard to do in such a traumatic place in life.

This is where I encourage you to get strong in your faith now, know what you know, and dig for what you do not know before trauma hits.

I did have my faith embedded even if not fully as God wanted it to be. But I had the foundation to know where to dig when my life collapsed.

Know what you know and put yourself in the place of growth in your faith walk.

Just because we think we know God has got this, it doesn't mean it's enough; we may need to do more than know it because someday, you may have to live in the knowledge of hope without the comfort of hope.

In 2012, I was dealing with both boys ages eighteen and twenty that trying to see where they wanted to be, not where they should or could be. It was all about them, what we should accept and how we should support them in their choices. There were numerous arguments about pot being okay, and if we would just accept that they were going to smoke pot, then we would have a great relationship.

Now I would have loved to support the choices we hoped they would be making by this time in their lives, like where to go to college, how to plan for their future, how to learn life skills and put them to use, but no, we didn't get to support those. We were asked to support their "drug" use, provide them funds to do and be where they wanted to be and accept their behavior as they saw fit.

They left us heartbroken and with additional financial brokenness. The more we offered guidance and help, the more they resisted and blamed us for getting in the way. However, they never gave up on the idea that we were to also support them financially in all they did.

If you are in the middle of a battle with your children, whether underage or adults, don't let them play on your heartstrings and make you feel you are the insane one, the hurtful one, and that if they "want it", then it should be okay. Not everything is okay, and it is okay to state that.

I started my 2012 journal with Psalm 46:10, "Be still and know that I am God." Writing it didn't' help my heart believe it. There would be much more needed from me before I could truly live in the scripture to be still and know that He is God.

Being still was and still is one of the hardest things for my body and mind to do but is so necessary.

That January, we received something good from our oldest. He brought home a small little puppy that we did not need but still have today as I am writing this.

She is the funniest biggest baby we have ever had, and she has brought us much laughter and joy while living in these struggles. We did not need or want another dog, but she filled a great spot within our family.

In April of 2020, we lost Sage to bone cancer. She was with us during all these hard years, and we loved her dearly. As we saw these last ten years come to an end and a new beginning take place, we heartbrokenly said goodbye to her.

Also, during those hard years, Oliver set it up for friends to come play games with us even though I did not think I was ready for that. These would be new friendships that still, today, I cherish. I would have rather stayed alone and worked on the why is and how is of our situation, but fortunately, God switched our personality roles during this time, and Oliver started creating friendships, activities, and fun things to do.

This, along with one of my dear friends wanting to get a bicycle for her fiftieth birthday and wanting us to get bikes as well started an activity of cycling which became my number one activity for all the following years to come.

God was planting seeds, activities, friendships, role changes in 2012 that I would see blossom, grow, and alternate the path we were on at the time.

Friends, faith, and fellowship, along with cycling and running, helped me through some of the toughest times of my life. And now that we are in a better place, these same things enhance and bless me even more now. I encourage everyone struggling find your "fun zone" even if it is way of out your "comfort zone". Out of our comfort zone is where we build strength and belief in ourselves.

In January 2012, I wrote that I just realized I needed a "Lisa" section in my journal first, then my sons. The real purpose in 2012 is to find myself again and pray for our sons but let go and let God deal with them.

I had said it before and will say it again many times in the next ten years to, let go and let God handle it, but that is so much easier said than done.

This would be about the time that I knew I had to work on me.

God was showing and teaching me many things during these years, and I needed to be the best and most aware of myself before I could be helped or healed. I had to want it to be better. I had to want to be helped and healed before I could let go as I needed to. Things started turning around for our oldest. He met with Reinhardt College and decided to attend there on a football scholarship.

I began a new Bible study by Beth Moore, James: Mercy Triumphs, and I began to hope for better days ahead.

The boys had both moved out, which is one of the most important steps in these situations. We parents are not supposed to support our young adult children in unhealthy situations. If they are not living healthy lives with you, it is time for them to provide for themselves.

We started feeling a peace that we had not had in a long time.

I know as parents we were never expected to have our adult-age children living under our roof not willing to follow our rules or our standards of living and disobedience. It was nice to sit at home without chaos and messiness under my feet.

And then I played scrabble with friends. That became a nightly go-to just to clear my mind of stress that invaded my day.

In January, we would attend a funeral of a young man we knew from our area that had lived with addiction until he took his own life. He was taken from this life way too early, along with others in his situation. I know the family and their love and support for him, his children, and other family members. He was loved greatly.

And then in February, Whitney Houston died, who had been struggling with addiction and abuse for so many years. She was so blessed and talented. She should have had what anyone would want in life, including wealth, unbelievable talent, beauty, a home, family that loved her, but addiction killed her.

I witnessed two deaths in the first two months of 2012 from addiction, and it was the extreme situations of a small-town guy, not known but loved, and then a very famous, beautiful, and wealthy singer that could have paid for any help she wanted but didn't. The only one change would have to be the changing of the heart, and the only way I know that can be changed is through the mercy and grace of God, when the battles we fight are so far beyond our control.

I was witnessing firsthand deaths of the same thing that my son was fighting which was addiction. And now ten years later, the death toll for addiction is now in the top causes of death with accidental death, suicide, and overdoses all from the opioid epidemic.

The Overdose Epidemic Drug overdose deaths continue to increase in the United States.

From Wikipedia,

The United States Centers for Disease Control and Prevention has data on drug overdose death rates and totals. Around 1,106,900 US residents died from drug overdoses from 1968 to 2020. Around 932,400 from 1999 through 2020. Around 91,800 in 2020. 28 people out of every 100,000 died from drug overdoses in 2020 in the US. Opioids were involved in around 80,400 of the around 106,700 deaths in 2021.

Around 110,500 people died in 2022. Around 109,900 people died in the 12-month period ending February 28, 2023, at a rate of 301 deaths per day.

Sadly, the overdose rate continues to grow.

So, I set my 2012 resolutions as:

1. Let go and let God, always a work in progress.

2. Travel to Montana and Wyoming to get out of the stressful environment. If possible, it is so important to step away even if just for a limited time.

3. Invest in properties because we would need to build up what we had lost while paying for all the cost of addiction.

4. Openness and willingness to talk about addiction and the effects it can have on the addict and the family. This is good for me and for others as well.

5. Our son to build skills. Find resources to better education, trade, and skills.

6. Our older son—college. We can't forget the needs of the other children.

7. Friends—continue to grow friendships. They are great in the good times and essential in the really bad times.

8. Play games and find humor in the hard times.

9. Save money and find a budget that works for you and try to explain and teach your children as well.

I tried to help others in their struggles, whether they are themselves or family members that struggled with addiction. I had many reach out to me for help or information, but what I found most of the time is that if it were the addict, they may say they wanted help or wanted change, but they didn't want it as much as they wanted the high. Or if it were the family member, they thought they wanted it but, in most cases, weren't willing to try something different.

If we are not willing to change, and if we do not believe we can be healed, then we waste our time just talking. You must want it, believe it can happen, give it over to God, and let God change us or them or all the above. We can talk all day, we can cry, get mad, fight, sit still, but the key is wanting to change more than where you are at the time and believing there is a way to be happy, healthy, and most importantly, healed!

This is not just for the addict; this is for everyone in whichever situation you are in. Do not become the victim. We were not created for that role.

As I saw in the year of 2012, if we do not take care of ourselves, we cannot help others, and our bodies, under tremendous stress, will begin to destruct. I felt like my entire body was suffering from some type of attack, whether it be my body, spirit, or mind. I was being attacked, and my physical body was starting to show signs.

During this year, I started to ride bicycles, play games with friends, putting any weight lost in the first year back on, and starting to breathe even if it were in short spurts.

What physical activity I began in 2012 has not only grown over the years but has given me a focus, a purpose to keep moving. It has helped me endure the extremely hard times where I have no control, and it began the healing process for my body, spirit, and mind. What I learned since 2012 is being used to help others within my community without me even realizing the road God was leading me to.

In April 2012, I had written in my journal, God's plan for me hit today. I will pray about it and make sure it is just "not me." Create a healthy community and bloom where I am planted instead of wanting to move to that.

From that time, life would move on, get harder with our son, and become more stressful. But God would use this time, without me recognizing it, to start building a platform on creating a healthy community.

As I write this now in 2020, I see so many areas where this has been happening, like being asked by the City of LaFayette to organize a local bicycle ride in 2016. This ride, the Honeybee Bicycle Ride, would give me a purpose to serve our community and in a very healthy way. I would be able to show off our community to other cyclists, raise money to help lower the fees for all LaFayette Recreation Department participants across all sports which, in turn, would allow all youth to participate at a more affordable rate.

I was able to connect with people within our county that would support and grow the healthy-living concept. Since this time, I have seen so much growth with initiatives like Walker Rocks, Bicycle Rides, Runs and Races, festivals, and true community growth in a fun and healthy lifestyle.

I had recently created a Run for God 5K Challenge and built on a Fit in Fit First platform, which encompasses an overall lifestyle of physical, mental, and spiritual health. If you had asked me in 2012 what I saw happening from all the trials and tribulations I would experience, I could not have imagined where I have "Fit In" with greater purpose in these last few years.

Now to Him who is able to do immeasurably more than all we ask or imagine, according to His power that is at work within us. (Ephesians 3:20 NIV)

CHAPTER 4

YEAR 2013

What Did We Do Wrong? Do You Want to Be Healed?

According to the Gospel of John, 9:3-5, Jesus saw a man who had been blind since birth. 3."Neither this man nor his parents sinned," said Jesus, "but this happened so that the works of God might be displayed in him. 4. As long as it is day, we must do the works of him who sent me. Night is coming when no one can work.

It is so easy to want to blame ourselves or our loved ones for something that has gone wrong in our lives. But it is not so easy to want to be healed no matter which side of the story you are on. We hold on to what we think we can control or what we believe we could never do, and we forget the main part of the story.

God is in control, and He uses all things for His good.

He uses our suffering to recognize our weaknesses and He shows us even when we make terrible choices, He can turn that around for good as well.

In the easiest times of my life, I sat in women's Bible studies not recognizing a future need, just enjoying the relationships that grew.

In the hardest times of life, I held onto what I had learned in women's Bible studies, and to the women who would pray and hold me up. And when I was on the other side of the trauma, hurt and heartache, I started sharing my story with others.

God had prepared my heart and mind so I would be prepared to help others when the time was right.

The time is right—for such a time as this! As was told to Ester, "For if you remain silent at this time, relief and deliverance for the Jews will arise from another place."

For if you remain silent at this time, relief and deliverance for the Jews will arise from another place, but you and your father's family will perish. And who knows but that you have come to your royal position for such a time as this? (Esther 4:14 NIV)

If for a time like this, I remain silent, relief and deliverance of those that suffer with what I had suffered in, could perish.

So, what do you mean when you say, "I want to be healed?" While struggling or suffering, we must ask ourselves, "do I really want to be healed?"

Do you really want it, and do you really believe it is possible?

Here are some scriptures that show all that was needed to be healed was to ask to be healed, believe they could be healed, and God healed them.

I pray we all might see with our eyes, hear with our ears, understand with our hearts, and turn and be healed. Heal me, Lord, and I will be healed; save me and I will be saved, for you are the one I praise. (Jeremiah 17:14)

Then Abraham prayed to God, and God healed Abimelek, his wife and his female slaves so they could have children again. (Genesis 20:17)

And the Lord heard Hezekiah and healed the people. (2 Chronicles 30:20)

Lord, my God, I called to you for help, and you healed me. (Psalm 30:2)

Make the heart of these people calloused; make their ears dull and close their eyes. Otherwise, they might see with their eyes, hear with their ears, understand with their hearts, and turn and be healed. (Isaiah 6:10)

The centurion replied, "Lord, I do not deserve to have you come under my roof. But just say the word, and my servant will be healed. (Matthew 8:8)

She said to herself, "If I only touch his cloak, I will be healed." (Matthew 9:21)

All it takes is to believe like the bleeding woman. It was the act of believing in just the touch of His garment and she could be healed.

We do not have to worry what is the right way to reach out to God; we just need to seek Him and ask to be healed. And if it is His will and, in His timing, we will be healed.

I would not know this in year four because I was still doing it my way and our son was still doing it his way and neither way was working.

We were not any closer to being "healed" than when we started, but the story was not over. I continued to feel like Job with no end in sight. My son and I would have a personal testimony of the healing power of Christ when we both surrendered to God's will and not our own. That still took several years for both of us.

Do not conform to the pattern of this world but be transformed by the renewing of your mind. Then you will be able to test and approve what God's will is, his good, pleasing, and perfect will. (Romans 12:2 NIV)

So, what did Year 4 of affliction look like for me?

This was the year I would search desperately for peace and comfort. I wanted to understand free will versus predestination, I needed to distance myself from drama, and embrace freedom and movement through cycling. I also focused on what 6:38 was telling me and why. I needed to find out what God was telling me through this sign. This was when I began to step out, search my heart, grow, and begin the journey God was setting out before me that I still didn't recognize at this time.

I applied to be the Specialized Road Bike Women's Ride Day leader for North Georgia. I had never done anything like this, but I applied and was picked to be that person. What an awesome opportunity to share the love of cycling and have the freedom to ride with over twenty-plus women within our community. And on that day, several of our husbands supported us with safety and SAG support along with a local bike shop helping and supporting. We were one group of happy and loved women on this day!

This was also the year that I would train to cycle a hundred-mile century ride. I had a friend that I was encouraging to do this with me, but her uncertainty of desire and ability was fluctuating, while mine never did. I was determined to do it, and we did, even with her uncertainties as I wrote about soon after we rode!

The Emotional Roller Coaster of a Century Bike

A cycling biography of a friend.

Me, Pre-Week: Are you going to do the Century?

My friend, "Apparently, and I want to see the Oreo cows."

And the rest is my friend!

Pre-Night: "I can't do the Century tomorrow."

Morning of: "Okay, I am going to try."

Mile 8: "This is great for the soul...the smells, flowers blooming, sights..."

Mile 40: No comment but thinking... I wonder if there is a way out of this.

Mile 50: Stopped and took pictures. We are halfway there. Feeling great! "I am doing this to see the Oreo cows."

Mile 60: "Lisa, I am so glad you encouraged me to do this. I hope we get to see the Oreo cows."

Mile 71: "I don't care if we stop to see the Oreo cows. If they are out, we will just look as we go by."

Mile 80: Break at Rutledge Downtown in the Gazebo…still feeling good. "I just need to put my feet up for a few minutes." This has been great.

Mile 81: "I don't care about the Oreo cows."

Mile 90: "I Will Never Do This Century Again."

Mile 99: Lisa says, "I need to stop and save my ride before my phone dies."

And my friend says, "I Am Not Stopping!"

Mile 101: She Did It, And.I.Knew.She.Could!

There were hard times, but then there were times like this that I was able to feel free, accomplished, and become totally exhausted from good times, not stressful times. I had just turned fifty, which was mentally one of the hardest years for me so far, but mixed with more peace, patience for myself, movement, friendships, and other opportunities God has placed before me.

There were other things that happened that put more stress into place in 2013. My dad had a heart attack while on the surgery table for gallbladder surgery. Fortunately, they recognized his problem was heart and not gallbladder before something deadly happened.

Once again, this is when we told our son it was time to move on. While my husband and I were enjoying a bicycle ride at the beach, we found out our son was arrested. When we got to the jail, we could only talk to him through glass, and it was heartbreaking to see him among grown men behind bars. I was once more at a loss of what to do and realized nothing I did was working.

The tension and fights between all of us continued, and he was arrested again back home within a month.

In May 2013, I attended my first ever AA meeting in Panama City Beach as a mother of an addict to see what these meetings were about. I wanted to learn everything that I could. It was amazingly enlightening, and I learned a lot from these people with their struggles and their faith. Some of the roughest-looking ones in the meeting were the kindest and most sincere ones and offered me future help if I needed it. The tattooed motorcycle brother was rough looking, but he gave me his phone number and said if I or my son ever needed help, to give him a call. He has "brothers" living all over the United States and would help us out anytime. Another man said, "It is a sickness, and we just have to change our thinking. Drinking makes us okay, popular, a John Wayne or a John Travolta, but we do not know how to stop. When it controls you, you cannot control it, and nobody understands that an alcoholic can't have just one." These AA members took me in and wanted to help me understand my son and his illness. I am so grateful for them. What a blessing.

Also, I was told during this time by someone that God has shown so much mercy for our son, that He must be planning on using him in some big way. It was words like these that gave me hope and encouragement in such a dark time.

On a positive note, in 2013, our other son was accepted at GSU, and we thought at least one of ours was on their way to gain their education. He did not stay but a year, but he began redirecting his life at that point, and we had released him fully to do that. That is the key, we must release our young adults to make their own choices whether good or bad choices, it is theirs to make at their expense and with their consequences that follow. That is one of the hardest things to do when you see them making the bad decisions, but the earlier they fail, the quicker they will learn from their consequences.

In August, we were celebrating our sons' last few days before going to GSU, and our younger son wanted to go to Chattanooga State and was excited, which was great news.

During 2013, as in many of the years to come, there would be a positive situation but then a terrible situation as well. Our emotions were riding a roller coaster that never stopped. I would also sign up for my first 5K in many years. I had not trained at all, but several of us went to walk, run, or just be together at this night run. It was wonderful, and I ran the entire 5K, which felt great until the next day when I was so sore that I could not walk.

There is a difference when you have prepared and think you can't, but you should try your best or instead, not prepare and think you can when you shouldn't.

I would also learn this lesson several more times over the next few years. And I am still learning that same lesson but recognizing it more now.

I took several trips to Panama City Beach in 2013. We owned a condo on the beach, and that is where I could go to reset if just for a few hours. The reset did not last long because the phone calls continued to come with added stress from all directions. But I did find a calm at the beach that I could not find anywhere else. It was the short trips, the bike rides, the runs, and the friendships that kept me moving during these incredibly hard years. However, stress finds its way to destroy your body, mind, and soul, and my body was showing the signs.

I was having extreme pain and stomach issues again, the second time since this started in 2010. I had a torn colon from stress again. The doctor said it was as if my colon had had a heart attack.

I do not remember having that much pain ever, and then my husband wrecked his bike on the Silver Comet Trail and had to be taken to hospital in Atlanta. I was on lots of pain meds for my torn colon, and he was in the emergency room with a possible broken hip, so my parents, in their late '70s and early '80s were driving me to Atlanta so I could be there for him.

This wasn't the first time my parents had to help us, and it would not be the last, but for now, they were driving us to doctors' appointments, work, and any other place we needed to be until one of us could drive again. There was something wrong with this picture. They ended up helping us and our kids when we should have been taking care of them, but that is not how it happened.

What I realized during this time and noted in my journal was "See, you really don't have any control and don't need to. I've got this, God. You have been out with illness for four weeks, and life for everyone has gone on."

And then my husband and I would start going to see a Christian counselor again. Things had to change, or we were not going to make it physically or mentally. Spiritually was all I had, but I needed the whole body, mind, and spirit to be working together, not just one part.

The torn colon got better, but then the nose bleeds began.

I was looking forward to a better year in 2014!

CHAPTER 5

YEAR 2014

The Lord replied, "My Presence will go with you, and I will give you rest."
—Exodus 33:14 (NIV)

I believe this scripture is not a coincidence since I was catching up on my Flourish Bible study Week 5, before starting to write this chapter of the year of 2014.

I did the study and then pulled all the files out for the year 2014, and the paper on top was a handwritten letter to God from me May 2014. Now what is also very intriguing is that I am getting ready today to leave for the beach again where I find peace, calm, and rest for my body, mind, and spirit.

The letter goes like this. (While at the beach)

Dear God,

This is where my mind and heart open, and I hear you more clearly. At home, it seems like chaos and confusion is all I feel.

Here, I can breathe, I feel Your presence, and I hear Your desires. Please, Lord, allow me to rest in Your presence and know what You want for me.

I am weak but use me for Your purpose. Lord, I need to be reminded to live where I am!

I need to bloom where I am planted. Show me how to do Your will. Place Your will for me into the desires of my heart so that I know the way to go.

Lord, help me let go of the things and people that I cannot help and give me strength to help the ones I can.

On the way to the beach, I could make a list of all the hurt each has done to me. Allow me to let go of these hurts and to look to You for comfort.

Show me how to turn all these things into glorifying You.

I see so much beauty here including the blue ocean, waves, birds, white sand, and I thank You for this.

Go with me and my family and guide us in the direction You desire. Fill our hearts with Your presence.

The Lord replied, "My presence will go with you, and I will give you rest." Exodus 33:14

Is it a coincidence that as I studied and wrote about this scripture this morning in my daily study, that as I packed and prepared to head to the beach in the morning with a dear friend, that I would tell someone that "I am in need of some R & R of body, mind, and soul, and I plan on doing nothing but reading, writing, and chilling," that God would place this letter and this study before me on this morning? Of course not.

He heard my need for guidance and direction, and He gave it to me, if only for a week. I will rest my body, mind, and soul in the presence of the Lord while treasuring the beautiful white sand and blue ocean. He is so gracious when we call on Him and for His will to be done.

Now let me be clear. My rest did not come in 2014, nor would it for several more years, but the rest I am searching for did come at many intervals along this journey, and I am in the process of finding it now.

The more fitting scripture for this year might be Isaiah 45:9–10.

Woe to the man who fights with his Creator. Does the pot argue with its maker? Does the clay dispute with him who forms it, saying, "Stop, you're doing it wrong!" or the pot exclaim, "How clumsy can you be?" Woe to the baby just being born who squalls to his father and mother, "Why have you produced me? Can't you do anything right at all?" Isaiah 45:9–10

In 2014, our son was at an all-time high literally and figuratively speaking, and our oldest decided to quit school and was engaged to be married within eight short weeks.

In May and June, we had a wedding to plan at our home for 150 and a rehearsal dinner to host at our home, while dealing with our youngest son's addictive choices.

Our son's first wedding shower was on June 1, 2014, just two weeks before the big day. All my dear girlfriends and their spouses were throwing an amazing shower to honor our son and his soon to-be wife.

Everyone was very excited, and it was the time to cherish the excitement and the celebrations happening for the soon-to-be wedding day.

Our youngest son would be his brother's best man and would have the honor in standing with and by him during this time, except for the fact that on that day, June 1, 2014, we received a message that we should check on our youngest to see if he was okay. He was asleep in his room, which was not unusual, but someone had heard he was knocked out the night before. When I went in and checked on him, he was totally out of it with dried blood that had come out his ears and his nose. And this was when the celebrations turned into chaos and trauma for all involved.

On June 2, 2014, as I was sitting in the hospital beside our youngest, I wrote, Routine…

What does routine mean?

It means nothing. Just because we think we have one, and some people like routine, we are not guaranteed routine, nor should we want to stay there.

My spiritual routine is to be in church on Sundays in addition to other Bible studies, but this Sunday, we went to a new (out of routine) Sunday school class that friends were teaching. The study was "good" about not getting stuck in life's routines that you miss hearing God, miss life's opportunities, miss a blessing or a calling, so the message was good, but only became clear within two hours of hearing it.

That was when our routine of going to church, coming home for lunch, deciding to work around the house or nap next changed. The rest of the day was spent getting our son to the hospital with possible head injuries, to distress, prayer, fear, anger, and all other emotions and actions involved when dealing with your child and serious injuries.

In the first hospital, My husband and I were standing quietly in his ER room, waiting for our son to come back from a brain scan when a person working in ER came by our room and asked if we needed anything. We said no, but we probably looked distressed. She asked if she could pray for us, and of course, we said yes. She walked into the room and surrounded us and prayed. We had not seen her before and have not seen her since, but what a blessing spiritually she was outside of our routine.

Routine may be going to Sunday School and hearing a lesson, but seeing and living in a life outside of routine is where you see the blessings.

I didn't know I would spend the next twenty-four hours in a trauma ICU waiting room, waiting on the news of our son's head injury, and I would never dream we would share this horrible experience with another family that had their son in the same trauma unit with head injuries and that we would have a connection through my cousin, one of the host, giving the wedding shower that night. My cousins sat between both families all night long and served and loved on us.

Nothing routine about the last twenty-four hours, but so blessed to be among friends, family, and now new connected friends that can pray, help, and sit with each other during this non routine event.

So, with one routine Sunday morning, I learned we have no routine. We may think we want routine, but life does not always give us routine, and thank God for that. Outside of routine is when we really feel God's Presence, witness His servants, and see their hearts. What a blessing that is during these traumatic situations.

I know God did not cause this to happen to our son and our family, but He worked in and through it. When we are outside of our routine, we can see more clearly God's hand and His people in it. I do not want illness and injury in our family, but I do want to remember that routine is not where I want to be! Routine is not sitting in a hospital room in the early morning writing this, but life is not routine and thank God for that!

May God bless our non-routine days!

There is this poem I had attached to this writing later.

The Road of Life

At first, I saw God as my observer,
my judge,
keeping track of the things I did wrong,
so as to know whether I merited heaven
or hell when I die.
He was out there sort of like a president.
I recognized His picture when I saw it,
but I really didn't know Him.
But later on
when I met Christ,
it seemed as though life was rather like a bike ride,
but it was a tandem bike,
and I noticed that Christ
was in the back helping me pedal.
I don't know just when it was
that He suggested we change places,
but life has not been the same since.
When I had control, I knew the way.
It was rather boring,
but predictable...
It was the shortest distance between two points.
But when He took the lead,
He knew delightful long cuts,
up mountains,
and through rocky places at breakneck speeds,
it was all I could do to hang on!
Even though it looked like madness,
He said, "Pedal!"
I worried and was anxious
and asked,
"Where are you taking me?"
He laughed and didn't answer,

and I started to learn to trust.
I forgot my boring life
and entered into the adventure.
And when I'd say, "I'm scared,"
He'd lean back and touch my hand.
He took me to people with gifts that I needed,
gifts of healing,
acceptance
and joy.
They gave me gifts to take on my journey,
my Lord's and mine.
And we were off again.
He said, "Give the gifts away;
they're extra baggage, too much weight."
So I did,
to the people we met,
and I found that in giving I received,
and still our burden was light. I did not trust Him,
at first,
in control of my life.
I thought He'd wreck it;
but He knows bike secrets, knows how to
make it bend to take sharp corners,
knows how to jump to clear high rocks,
knows how to fly to shorten scary passages.
And I am learning to shut up and pedal
in the strangest places,
and I'm beginning to enjoy the view
and the cool breeze on my face
with my delightful constant companion, Jesus Christ.
And when I'm sure I just can't do anymore,
He just smiles and says…
"Pedal."

(Author Unknown)

And for me, 2014 was the year I just needed to pedal. I needed to pedal through the hard stuff, the struggles with both my son's choices, good and bad. I needed to forget what was behind and hold onto the new life one day at a time, one pedal stroke at a time, and enjoy the view, the cool breeze on my face and the constant companion, Jesus Christ, who would be with me every step of the way.

And that year, I would also ride through life literally on the seat of a bike learning along the way. I put a lot of hard miles on my heart in 2014, and I put a lot of miles on my bike as well.

In reflecting back over 2014 while in 2020, I had written a couple of quotes from Choosing to SEE by Mary Beth Chapman:

Even the saddest things can become, once we have made peace with them, a source of wisdom and strength for the journey that still lies ahead.

May this be your experience; may you feel the Hand which inflicts the wound, supplies the balm, and that He who has emptied your heart has filled the void with Himself.

And I ended this writing in 2014 with 1 Peter 5:10.

And the God of all grace, who called you to his eternal glory in Christ, after you have suffered a little while, will himself restore you and make you strong, firm, and steadfast. 1 Peter 5:10 NIV

CHAPTER 6

YEAR 2015

I can do everything through Him who gives me strength. Philippians 4:13

This was my hope starting in 2015.

I would like to give you a glimpse of what my husband and I do at the end of each year. We list resolutions for the following year or top five things we want to do in that upcoming year.

Ours are always quite different from each other's because I take it seriously, and he usually makes up something absurd and unrealistic.

Top 5 Things I Want to Do in 2015

1. Take a great summer trip—Colorado.
2. Do something needed and important for others.
3. Do an outstanding accomplishment—maybe a Half IRONMAN?
4. Find my home church.
5. Find peace in the storms.

We did take big trips out of the country and to Colorado plus several smaller trips. I worked on events for others. God planted the seed within me for the IRONMAN that I would accomplish in 2018. I eventually found my home church, but until I did, I met many new friends that I still have today, and on occasion, I found peace in the storms. And we were blessed with our first grandbaby which tops them all!

Lisa J. Heyer

My husband:

1. Quit work.
2. Race in the Tour de France
3. Gain twenty pounds of muscle.
4. Shave body.
5. Get a tattoo.

My husband didn't quit work, nor has he yet. He has never and will never race in the Tour de France. He did gain weight but not muscle, and he didn't shave his body or get a tattoo.

During these times of setting our goals and especially when you live in a crisis for many years, it is always important to get time away to let go of what is and have some fun, even if it is to plan what isn't realistic. We have had lots of laughs over his list, and that is just about as important on the to-do list as anything.

By year 2015, I was thinking that our journey through addiction should be coming to an end. A dear friend of mine had said her son's addiction stopped in five years when he got older and out of the teenage years, so in the back of my mind, that was our plan too.

That did not happen! Starting in Year 5 of his addiction, I stopped writing as much. The stories are dim, and the only real memories are the few I have written down. I was having to help our son detox off drugs. I was given instructions on how to give him a total of 40 mg, and I don't even remember what, but taking him from 40 mg to 30 mg to 20 mg to 10 mg to 5 mg to 3.5mg to 2.5 mg over a five-week period. I could not believe I was having to track and provide our son with the drugs he needed on a schedule. This goes against anything I would have ever believed I would need to do for my son, much less being for an addiction condition.

This was during March through April of 2015, and after that, not much changed. We went through all that, walked into a Suboxone clinic which appeared to be a legalized drug-dealer clinic. I did not agree with this, and now I am glad I did not.

When I asked the doctor how long he would be on Suboxone for the detox, the doctor stated it could be for a lifetime. That was not detoxing; that was just changing addictions, and I was not going for that, so we walked out. Our son was an addict. We did not need to change drugs; we needed to be healed and healthy!

During this year, I was still fighting against his addictions, but I also was cherishing the time with our first grandchild from our other son. Talking about emotions going from high to low, it was a constant roller coaster, but I never gave up on praying for our son, but I did try to put more energy into the positive.

We had a busy year with a trip to Germany to see family, baby showers, camping, weddings, arrival of first grandson, bike rides, Bible studies, and a trip out west to Colorado. I filled my time with activities and events that kept me busy and my mind occupied. I was learning again to find freedom within the chaos.

In September and October of that year, I wrote out prayers while our son lived in Colorado, once again trying to find himself. Instead, he found harder drugs.

September 29, 2015

Dear heavenly Father,

You say you are not far from us, for in You we live, move, and exist. I pray desperately that You get as close to our son as You can. Let him feel Your presence. Give him the vision to see Your presence, plan, and power over his many obstacles.

Dear Lord, guide him right where he belongs. I know and believe You and trust that Your plan is greater than either of ours.

October 1, 2015

As our son drives back from Colorado one more time…

Dear heavenly Father, I pray You will protect our son on his travels and allow him to feel Your presence while he is driving all these miles.

Place the desire in his heart to look to You and to be ready for a real transformation and restoration of the body, mind, and soul. Use me and guide me in this so that he is healed, and You are glorified.

Give my husband and me the tools and patience needed for this task.

In Jesus's name I pray.

Scripture on the bottom of the journal on this day:

He made us, and we are His. We are His people, the sheep of His pasture. Psalm 100:3

So, knowing our son was on his way back home, I did what comes naturally which is to start planning.

In hindsight, this is about the time I started connecting goals to sobriety with body, mind, and soul.

Goals First Thirty days Sobriety:

1. Get expert help.

2. Stay away from friends and peer groups.

3. Go to church.

4. Surround yourself with those that care and are clean (in all ways).

Sobriety means restraint from everything—drugs, alcohol. and weed.

Getting mind, body, and soul back into shape:

1. Train the body through running, biking, and/or swimming with accountability.

2. Retrain mind—counseling and therapy.

3. Train spiritually with music, prayers.

Scripture on the bottom of the journal on this day:

Give your burdens to the Lord, and He will take care of you. Psalm 55:22

I continued to work on ideas and plans in my notebook.

Sober:

sobriety
other skills
body
exercise
restore

You, to become who You were meant to be!

And I created a "lesson plan" for him to work on:

First admit you are weak, wrong and a wreck then allow yourself to be restored.

Work on body, mind, and soul

For body, exercise.

For mind, sobriety and get started with help.

For soul, read Wild at Heart by John Eldridge.

Other items: check for school deadlines, registrations, and degrees available.

Projects and work to complete.

home maintenance
budgets
faith
finance
organization

Scripture on the bottom of the journal on this day:

God blesses those who work for peace, for they will be called the children of God. Matthew 5:9

And then he should retreat, rest, renew, and restore. He was to identify the issues, set a plan of action, start moving forward, and determine resources for all issues.

Scripture on the bottom of the journal on this day:

Anything is possible if a person believes. Mark 9:23

Throughout October, I wrote more prayers.

On October 7, 2015:

Dear heavenly Father, It is apparent that we need guidance and patience with our son. I am trying to meet him where he is instead of where I want him to be. I pray I can be for him what I need to be and direct him back to You. I want to glorify You in this and as I have been studying, I know You are the only One that can satisfy his inner soul.

Every time he thinks or says Your name, fill him with your presence and full satisfaction. Be so near to him that he knows something is special and different. Then give me that too!

The scripture on the bottom of the journal on this day:

Blessed are those who trust in the Lord and have made the Lord their hope and confidence. Jeremiah 17:7

On October 12, 2015:

Dear heavenly Father, You say to trust in You with all my heart and lean not on my own understanding, in all my ways submit to You and You will make my path straight.

I pray you will do that for me. I need the path to become clear in recognizing my place and the place of those around me in work and home.

Use me.

Open and close the doors but lead me with Your light and with wisdom. I know if I do Your will, I will be blessed and feel the satisfaction while glorifying You too.

Scripture on the bottom of the journal on this day:

Come to Me, all of you who are weary and carry heavy burdens, and I will give you rest. Matthew 11:28

I wrote a couple of other prayers, but then I wrote a letter to myself.

Dear Younger Me,

After writing what my strongholds are, I think it is good to write myself a letter.

If I could start over, I would go against the norm of success and find the radically unconventional way—decrease instead of increase!

I would decrease any amount of control I thought I had and understand God is able.

I would recognize perfection is not perfect, only God is.

When trying to help someone close to me, I would not take on the burden without God's will and His guidance. It would be too much to carry alone.

When it comes to work and busyness, I would search for your expectations, not my own or what others expect from me. You are the only one that sees the big picture. I would listen to You and my body for what it needs, not what I desire. Accomplishments are not always accomplishments when they rule your health.

Everything in moderation, especially physical exercise. I would be more aware of my emotional sobriety—stop identifying with the emotional pain and calmly relate to it with compassion.

Ask the question, what caused this to happen versus why they did this to me!

I would identify any bitterness before it takes root. Name it and turn it over to God. Recognize God has this! I do not have to make it right.

And finally, decrease outside desires.

Do not let them own me, just enjoy them. There is much freedom in less. Less distractions, less responsibilities, less stress, less maintenance. Everything we add, adds something to manage, repair, fix, and pay for.

Most importantly, God first!

Remember who brought me here and find out for what!

How can I glorify God in all this life?

Scripture on the bottom of the journal on this day:

No eye has seen, no ear has heard, and no mind has imagined what God has prepared for those who love Him. (1 Corinthians 2:9) What has amazed me the most while looking back and writing this from 2015 is that in every page I wrote, prayed, and set plans, God finished with a preprinted scripture at the bottom of each page for such a time as this. We may miss a beat or two, but God does not.

And I will add.

Revelation 1:3:

Blessed is the one who reads aloud the words of this prophecy and blessed are those who hear it and take to heart what is written in it, because the time is near. Revelation 1:3

and

Matthew 13:15–16: For this people's heart has become calloused; they hardly hear with their ears, and they have closed their eyes. Otherwise, they might see with their eyes, hear with their ears, understand with their hearts and turn, and I would heal them. But blessed are your eyes because they see, and your ears because they hear. Matthew 13:15–16

CHAPTER 7

YEAR 2016

A Year of Blurs, Arrest, and Lots of Prayers

Rejoice always, pray continually, give thanks in all circumstances; for this is God's will for you in Christ Jesus. 1 Thessalonians 5:16–18 NIV

I found in looking back into 2016 that I did not write a lot. I had written a few prayers and notes which I will include, but nothing is clear except that our son was still struggling terribly, had been arrested, and was back in a rehab facility at Ridgeview in Atlanta. In addition, my mother-in-law had an unforeseen hospital experience which took her life within a few months, and which would entail a three-week trip to Europe.

These things along with everyday life, work, and stress would keep my emotional roller coaster on full speed.

So, I rode my bicycle!

During this time, all my favorite things started with B's.

Bible study, biking, books, boys (mine), beach, and best friends…not in order!

Hobbies to keep me moving mentally and physically were travelling, eating, and biking! I have a lot of energy and love movement. On January 21, 2016, I read the devotional from Jesus Calling Morning, and it said,

"I want you to be all mine. I am weaning you from other dependencies. Your security rests in Me alone, not in other people, not in circumstances."

The verses that went along with this day's devotion were Deuteronomy 33:27, Proverbs 16:9, and Romans 8:38–39.

The eternal God is your refuge, and underneath are the everlasting arms. He will drive out your enemies before you, saying, "Destroy them!" Deuteronomy 33:27 NIV

In their hearts, humans plan their course, but the Lord establishes their steps. Proverbs 16:9 NIV

For I am convinced that neither death nor life, neither angels nor demons, neither the present nor the future, nor any powers, neither height nor depth, nor anything else in all creation, will be able to separate us from the love of God that is in Christ Jesus our Lord. Romans 8:38–39 NIV

All these verses at the beginning of a new year helped me put the kickoff of 2016 into clearer prospective. God is my only refuge; the Lord will establish my steps, and nothing in all creation will be able to separate me from the love of God that is in Christ Jesus, our Lord.

During the last few years, the number 6:38 kept coming to me, but in 2016, it started looking different to me. In the scripture Luke 6:38, "pressed down, shaken together and running over," looked like the "shaken" became my scattered. Our family that was all in one cup was shaken like dice and scattered. Each of us had a different route to take, our own journey, that only God knew.

How do we use #638 and feel as if we are doing something?

Give, and it will be given to you. A good measure, pressed down, shaken together, and running over, will be poured into your lap. For with the measure you use, it will be measured back to you. Luke 6:38 NIV

And then Psalm 46:10 says, "Be still and know that I am God."

April 26, 2016

Dear heavenly Father,

I thank you for the words you give me in scripture. Rejoice always, pray continually, give thanks in all circumstances; for this is God's will for you in Christ Jesus. 1 Thessalonians 5:16–18 NIV.

This scripture is comforting to "be joyful always, pray continually, give thanks in all circumstances for this is God's will for you in Christ Jesus." In these difficult times, I need to remember You have this, and You have me.

Control is bondage that when released allows so much freedom. Thank you for helping me understand that it is not mine to fix. And Dear Lord, please help others understand it is not mine to fix too.

This would be a constant petition because when everyone is used to me being in control and "fixing things", they continue to expect it even when it is out of my control totally.

Go with our son and give him the desire to get there. Lead him. He is Your child that struggles and suffers, and we do not know what to do anymore.

I pray this in Your name, Amen.

May 1, 2016, 7:00 a.m.

Dear heavenly Father,

Thank you for this down time with friends at the campground. I pray my husband feels good about coming home and renewing of relationships when he leaves Germany.

I pray for healing and wisdom for all on behalf of his mom.

Lord, I pray for our son this upcoming week. Prepare his heart and his mind. Give him Your peace that passes understanding. Let him feel Your presence.

And Lord, prepare my heart and soul and direct my path in the direction of Your will. In that, I know, it will bring freedom.

Use me and direct me.

Guide me in preparing Walker County Cities on our Knees.

Lead me in the direction You want me to go.

In Your name I pray. Amen.

July 6, 2016, at my husband's parents' house in Germany while visiting the hospital in his mom's last days, there is peace in seeing all the children/ siblings come back together. I pray for these people in Germany. I see churches, cathedrals, and even statues of Jesus Christ, but I do not see the faith.

I hear church bells all night long in the village, but the people seem lost and unhappy.

Why? How can one be in an area with so much history of faith and yet having no faith?

Maybe like the USA, it is turning "we trust" into being now governed by "whatever goes is good."

Will we look back in ten, twenty, one hundred years and have churches, church bells, statues of Jesus Christ but no faith?

Just in the past four years since writing this prayer, I have seen our country get further from the Truth and faith that was our country's foundation to whatever goes, goes. But now in 2020, will the COVID-19 pandemic lead us back to our foundation? Not yet, but I pray it will. Time will tell.

Can anyone say our country is the same as before? If not, what changed? If acceptance of all is good, why are we living in such a corrupt and dark time? When we had standards, boundaries, and expectations, we were a proud country. But just like a child with no boundaries, we get out of control. With all the political corruption and uncertainty, I wonder where we are headed.

I pray that we begin to have believers with boundaries in our government offices and all leadership before we get to the point of no return.

In September 2016, I had written that I was thinking of writing a compiled book from transformations that were still transforming. It would be called Scattered, Smothered, and Yet Covered, and I had this extremely limited layout.

The title came to me on June 18, 2013, before a book was ever written, and before the story unfolded in the years to follow.

Chapter 1: Scattered in 2010

Chapter 2: the in-betweens, The Journey Chapter

3: Smothered—Can't Breathe and In and Out for Seven Years The emotions, highs, and lows like a storm—from calm, storm to beauty, and the Lesson's Learned.

Chapter 4: Covered Through it All—Veiled in His Presence.

Dark times—travels to Europe and felt like sitting in the desert for three weeks while visiting in this dark presence of Germany, but still finding peace in His presence.

Living to glorify Him, which was my original goal but did not know how that looked until He brought me through it throughout the years to follow.

I had just written, "Lord use me and make my path clear". Something that I still write and pray for all the time.

October 24, 2016

O Lord, the great and awesome God, heavenly Father, the Most High above all, blessed be Your name, Your kingdom come, please, sooner than later.

Heavenly Father help me reach those that still question You and their faith.

Dear heavenly Father, give each of us our daily needs so that our focus and praise can be on You and Your will.

Father, forgive me and forgive all the United States of America for our sins. We have been so spoiled that we forget that You have blessed us all tremendously. We have been given much, and much we should give.

We have all sinned and fallen terribly short of righteousness.

And because You have forgiven us, we shall also forgive everyone who sins against us. Those that have wronged us or sinned against us are nothing in comparison to our continued sin and independence of you, Lord. Forgive us and help us forgive others.

Heavenly Father, lead us away from temptations. We are not able to handle or recognize all temptations, but You are God and in control over all things. You are the Most High God over all kingdoms, all kings, all people, all animals, heaven and earth.

You reign!

Protect us, guide us, forgive us, help us be like You created us to be.

Amen.

October 25, 2016

I pray as Daniel prayed when he was heartbroken over the people's sinful nature and the sins of his people and nation. I pray to the Lord, my God, and confess that we have sinned and done wrong. We have been wicked and have rebelled; we have turned away from Your commands and laws. We have not listened to Your servants, the prophets.

Lord, You are righteous, but this day we are covered with shame—the people of America and the world have been unfaithful to You. O Lord, we and our leaders are covered in shame because we have sinned against You. The Lord our God is merciful and forgiving even though we have rebelled against You. We have not obeyed the Lord, our God or kept the laws He gave us through His servants, the prophets. We have transgressed Your law and turned away, refusing to obey You.

Now, O Lord our God, hear the prayers and petitions of Your servant. For Your sake, O Lord, look with favor on Your desolate sanctuary. Give ear, O God, and hear. Open Your eyes to this desolation of our country. We do not make requests because we are righteous but because of Your great mercy.

O Lord, listen, O Lord, forgive! O Lord, hear and act! For Your sake, O my God, do not delay because Your people bear Your name.

October 26, 2016

Perseverance must finish its work so that you may be mature and complete, not lacking anything. James 1:4

Dear heavenly Father, our Protector and Father,

You have blessed us and protected us more than we deserve.

Our family cares, loves, and has suffered much through our son's struggles.

I have persevered and can see the building of my character. I just pray that I can see our son in a better place.

He is Your child, and You say You will never leave us or forsake us, so I beg You to work on our son. Direct his heart, soul, and mind to You. Our son is a beautiful young man with such a heavy, hurting heart. It is one that only You, the Healer, can reach.

Lord, I lay him at Your feet. He is all Yours.

Amen.

Jesus Calling/Evening, said, "Look up to Me and see My Face shining down on you!" I looked, and I saw!

And then I had a vision of Jesus Christ looking at me through my heart painting which hangs in my sunroom/writing room.

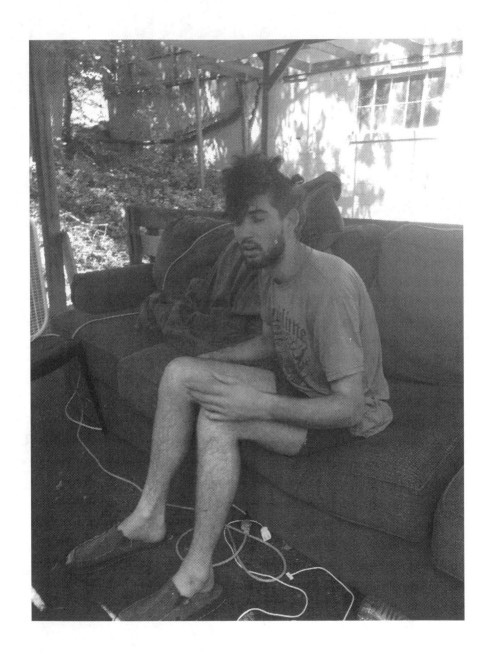

CHAPTER 8

YEAR 2017

Though He brings grief, He will show compassion, so great is His unfailing love. Lamentations 3:32 NIV

This year seemed to be one of the hardest. There was more fighting, more arrests, stealing, lying, and in July 2017, our son was homeless, jobless, and using more than ever. There was no end in sight.

About this time, I came across "An Open Letter from an Addict" which says what is happening in the heart and mind of an addict and, at the time, my son.

An Open Letter from an Addict (Author Unknown but sent to us from an addiction rehab)

To Those Who Suffer with Us and because of Us

First, you need to know that my addiction is not your fault. It's nothing you did or did not do.

Mom, it's not because you worked so much or didn't have dinner with me every night.

Dad, it's not because you drank too much or remarried too soon.

Brother or sister, it's not because you took away my spotlight.

Husband, wife, partner, lover…it's not because you told me I was fat or not smart enough or not good enough or chose her over me.

No, it's none of these reasons.

You need to understand that my addiction is not your fault. Repeat that. Roll it over and over in your mind. My addiction is not your fault. In fact, it's not yours at all. It is mine.

Secondly, please stop asking me why I am doing this to you. Addiction is not a weapon…it isn't something we choose to wield against those we love; it isn't suppressed anger or aggression in the form of a pill or a needle or a pipe. You must understand… I don't know why I am doing this to myself, much less you. Even more… I don't care what I'm doing to you. I care about the pill…or the needle…or the pipe. And that is all.

My life is a drug of choice. It controls me, consumes me, dictates all my thoughts and actions with absolutely no regard to consequences or outcome. And this includes hurting you.

I don't understand what hurting someone means anymore… I am blind to your feelings, deaf to your pleas, numb to any emotion you may be feeling. I do not feel anything. I feel sick when I am not high, and I feel a distorted sense of normal when I am. But you see…

I cannot be high and have the human experience of emotion at the same time. I am a shell. I have no capacity to love or hate or cry or feel anything at all. I am a shell, fueled by pills only to find and use more pills. Your concerns are none of my concerns.

I will lie to you and steal from you and deny, deny, deny. And somewhere, deep down inside, I know I am hurting you, killing you even…and this little part of me hates the rest of me for all that I am doing, but the drugs are so loud, **Deafening Sounds in My Mind**, and they always win.

I will leave you lying, battered, and beaten and begging me to stop, on my well-worn path of self-destruction and never look back, as long as the outcome is drugs coursing through my veins.

This is not your fault. And I don't destroy you because I don't love you. I destroy you because the drugs are destroying me and I can't stop, won't stop, don't know how to stop.

I lie in bed at night and pray to a god that I don't think exists that I will not repeat the cycle tomorrow… but God doesn't answer. The drug answers, and they tell me the only escape is more, more, more, always more. And I believe them.

My addiction is not yours. It is mine. It is my prison, it is my god, it is my heaven and my hell, my lover, my enemy, my only companion. I do not want it but cannot rid myself of it. You cannot help me. You cannot love me out of it, hate me out of it, buy me or bribe me out of it. I am the only one holding the key to my own dungeon, yet I cannot find the locked door for the darkness.

Not until I have had enough pain, enough loss, enough misery, enough…, will I try to change. But when I do, my climb out of my grave will be my own. It has to be my own because only then will I value that climb, that pain, that change.

Please be patient with me. This change is not an easy one, or a fast one, or even a guaranteed one. The wreckage that I have left will not disappear overnight.

Please do not push me to fix it all right now. It took years to destroy my life, and while I am trying my best, I will not repair it all before tomorrow's dawn.

My addiction is not yours. No matter how well you know me, how much you love me, you do not know the addiction that rages inside of me.

It looks nothing like the daughter or son or brother or sister or husband or wife or lover you know. No, you do not know the voice in my head that convinces me to disregard you and your love. That tells me to find it, find that pill, then find that needle and put it in my arm and forget about you and the pain in your eyes.

I fight daily to speak louder, think smarter, be braver than this voice. This battle is my own.

You cannot help me fight it. My addiction is not yours. It is mine.

And today, I have silenced it. Today, I feel love for you. Today, I am grateful for you. Today, I choose to be the person you know and love and understand.

My addiction is my own. And today, just for today, I have won.

The year 2017 was a continuous battle with our son and his actions. We were at a loss and had to find our way in all this once again. It hurt, and there was little to no hope. But the story wasn't over, and God wasn't done with any of us.

Our son went once again to another rehab, and then with a big twist in all our stories, he ended up in Franklin, North Carolina, at Men's Teen Challenge of the Smokies. What seemed like the rock bottom ended up being the place of healing, hope, and recovery in the year to come.

Once our son was admitted in the program at Teen Challenge, we were able to breathe and begin to live again. These are the days and nights that you feel they are safe even if not healed.

Throughout this year, we had to continue to work, live, and do life, but now we could do it with less stress on our minds about whether our son was safe somewhere and still alive.

So, I worked, planned events, and rode…

I found peace by riding bikes. I wrote that,

I ride because of Relationships!

1. I am connected in a way with God while riding in so many ways! I see the beauty, feel His presence as I listen to Christian music, pass deer, bald eagles, see mountains and valleys and much more. I see His blessings!

2. My husband rides, so I enjoy that relationship where we have something that we share! We share the enjoyment of riding, even if not at the same time or same pace. Our love for biking has given us a common love of this activity!

3. I love the relationship with my friends who ride with me most days! Sometimes we talk and laugh the whole ride, and other days we ride without saying much out of the need to just be, but whatever we are doing that day, we love each other and love being in that moment with a friend!

4. I love my relationship with my older teenage boys because I ride! If I did not ride and get my energy out on my bike, I might kill them some days!

5. And last, but not least, I ride for my relationship with myself! While riding, I find myself, my passion, my peace, my endurance, and my desire to push myself in ways that otherwise would not be. I gain the freedom to be me and push myself without affecting anyone else, except my girlfriends who ride with me.

I only started riding less than two years ago and will turn fifty next week. My only regret is that I didn't find out the joy of riding earlier but feel blessed to know it now, and I began riding several long rides that year, including Brag a four-hundred-mile ride and a few fifty to one hundred miles! So, thanks to my riding, all my relationships are stronger, appreciated, and loved more!

I have gained many more friendships and have traveled across Georgia on a bike with twenty-plus new local friends and with another eight hundred-plus people I enjoyed for the week. I have formed long and lasting relationships with people all over the state. I have also traveled across the country and ridden my bike in all the cities along the way.

I have learned that communities across our nation are embracing the health and exercise culture through biking, and those cities that embrace it create an environment people like to live and travel in.

I have learned a lot about myself and so many other cyclists like me.

It is about the peace and passion you feel when riding and the excitement of seeing new places and faces along the way. We all have our problems such as grief, fear, sickness, diseases, losses, but we all recognize the blessings we have and share together.

My newest desires and goal were to help create this environment in our hometown of LaFayette and all of Walker County. I was thrilled when I was contacted by the City of LaFayette to see if I would be interested in helping create a biking event.

It is my passion to see our community grow in a positive way that betters the lives of children, families, and community. What an Awesome Opportunity!

And so, in 2017, I began my year planning for the first City of LaFayette community bicycle ride.

God gave me a platform to work from that I loved and could sink my heart into. When God calls you to do something, take the opportunity! You will be blessed in many ways.

I would be creating a community bicycle ride, the Honeybee Bicycle Metric-Century Ride, and in our first year, we would have approximately 150 riders. The event would raise money for our local recreation department to reduce registration fees for every activity so that more families could participate and support the youth in our community.

This took my love for our young people like my own son, the opportunity to broaden their outdoor exercise and activities in a positive manner, along with my love of cycling, and put it together to give back to our community. #638

And it was truly a Luke 6:38 event. I was able to give, and it was given back to me in many ways. I was thrilled and blessed to be a part of this new adventure in our community. I did not come up with the idea, but I was blessed to be included in the planning and orchestrating of it. Helping others and our community allowed me to release our son more and more to himself. I could put my energy and hope into our community, our people, and help locally when my help for my child was not working.

I was learning to let go more and more. Redirect the focus from the addiction or addict is very important.

In 2017, I was "pressing toward the goal", but wasn't sure what that goal looked like.

This was a terribly hard year but one that would start change in our lives and in our sons.

As Paul says in Philippians, "Not that I have already obtained all this, or have already arrived at my goal, but I press on to take hold of that for which Christ Jesus took hold of me. Brothers and sisters, I do not consider myself yet to have taken hold of it. But one thing I do: Forgetting what is behind and straining toward what is ahead, I press on toward the goal to win the prize for which God has called me heavenward in Christ Jesus." Philippians 3:12– 14 NIV

Following Paul's example,

"All of us, then, who are mature should take such a view of things. And if on some point you think differently, that too, God will make clear to you. Only let us live up to what we have already attained. Philippians 3:15–16

CHAPTER 9

YEAR 2018

"Reckless Love"

"I will feed My flock and I will lead them to rest," declares the Lord God. "I will seek the lost, bring back the scattered, bind up the broken and strengthen the sick; but the fat and the strong I will destroy. I will feed them with judgement." Ezekiel 34:15–16

October 27, 2018, our son successfully completed the twelve-month program at Teen Challenge of the Smokies, but more than that, he was sober, recovered, healed, and happy.

This did not come suddenly when he arrived at Teen Challenge in 2017. It would take months before he surrendered himself to the program and, more importantly, to God. It is only through the "reckless love of God" that our son surrendered as he shared in his testimony.

As the song says in Reckless Love Song by Cory Asbury

Before I spoke a word, You were singing over me

You have been so, so good to me

Before I took a breath, You breathed Your life in me

You have been so, so kind to me

Oh, the overwhelming, never-ending, reckless love of God

Source: LyricFind

Teen Challenge of the Smokies Men's Center, October 2018

Our son's testimony.

The Reckless Love of God

I shouldn't be writing this. I should be dead or in jail. It's only by the reckless love of God that I'm able to tell you, my story. I am twenty-four years old now, and I've been in addiction for eight years. My addiction progressed very fast from when I was fifteen, only smoking weed, to at age eighteen being addicted to prescription opiates. Between those years, I was sent away to multiple mental hospitals/rehabs. I would cry myself to sleep and was so angry at my parents for sending me away. I became so lost and broken during my addiction. I felt hopeless thinking that I would be a drug addict for the rest of my life.

I tried moving away a few times and admitted myself into a few secular rehabs. I moved to Colorado to try and get off painkillers and found myself addicted to meth. I soon moved back to Georgia to get help but then remained addicted to meth and opiates. Stealing and manipulating my family and friends became a daily habit to get high. I got caught stealing some guns and jewelry from my family and had a choice to either face charges or go to a year-long rehab. (And yes, we threatened that and that is when his life started to change.)

I came to Teen Challenge after some wild events happened, and there I was, standing at Teen Challenge, suicidal and lost, not sure what I wanted from life and not sure if I could ever quit doing drugs. I wanted to change but wasn't sure how that looked. I really couldn't imagine life without drugs.

I had been fighting this God thing my whole life. I would tell myself there wasn't a God because if there was, and He actually loved me, then I wouldn't feel the way I did. My entire life I was seeking the wrong things to try and fill that emptiness that only God can fill. God is so real. He has given me peace that I cannot explain. He has given me hope and a future just like it promises in Jeremiah 29:11.

I never thought our God was a tangible God, but He is. He sent us Jesus the author and finisher of our faith. He also gave us His Word, which has become a blessing to my heart. I'm beginning to trust in God more each day because I truly do believe that He will never forsake me.

I hope that people can see Jesus in me and that He still saves and heals.

And this was just the written testimony. Our son gave one of the best live testimonies I have ever witnessed. You can view it on my website, LisaHeyer.com.

Maybe because he is my son, but more because I had lived firsthand in the desperate and destructive life, he had been living for the last eight years. I lived this testimony.

"I have told you these things so that in me you may have peace. In this world, you will have trouble. But take heart. I have overcome the world." John 16:33

In 2018, I felt God leading me to sign up for IRONMAN Chattanooga 70.3. I knew it had to be God because I physically wasn't prepared to do anything of such magnitude. I hadn't been running, I hadn't ever used swimming as a sport except for playing in a pool, and I had never competed in a cycling event. I had only cycled in rides, not races, so this desire was not from me. It was from someone much bigger than me. It was all God!

During this time, I was journaling all I was experiencing while training, like my fears, pain, struggles, and wrote how God showed me through songs and signs throughout my training, why I needed to continue this endurance training.

I started seeing the correlation between my training for such a huge endurance race to our son's training for healing from addiction. This was when the first thought of writing a book called Endurance Race of Life and Addiction began.

All along I thought that someday I would write my story of addiction, but I never dreamed God would use such a platform as IRONMAN to teach me lessons about myself and help me see and feel some of the challenges my son was facing in his journey with addiction at the same time.

I wrote my first book, Endurance Race of Life and Addiction, in 2018–2019, and it was published by Christian Faith Publishing in 2019.

I included this in the book:

> This is written for my son and all those that struggle with addiction. Addiction must be the worst stronghold anyone faces. While our country fights the epidemic of opioids, so many of our families are losing their battles to overdoses, deaths, and mental health illnesses. This needs to stop.
>
> To the families of those addicted, I encourage you to find your role in your family members' addiction. Do not enable, disable, or just tolerate. You have a role to play, and it can be a healthy, loving role with many rewards, including a healthy, happy, and hopeful family member and a successful recovery someday.
>
> Also, this is written for all the women out there that hit their mid-fifties and think they are "too old" to do anything active. Do not believe those lies. The devil would like to keep you right where you are. Think again! When your desire to be better becomes hard, push through it and do it anyway! You will love the results.
>
> And for any of you that have ever wanted to complete or compete in a race, a bike ride, a 5K, 10K, or an

IRONMAN, go for it. Step out in faith, get moving, and when it is hard, do it anyway!

There is hope. Do not stop fighting.

The battle is real, but there is hope; hope to win the race. This endurance race for life is not easy, but it is available to you. God has a plan for you and me. Be willing to work His plan.

There is freedom waiting for you there.

In sincere love, faith, and hope,

Lisa Heyer

Not only did God give me an amazing platform to write about, but then He opened doors that would allow me to speak to those struggling and the families and friends that struggle with them. I have spoken to the participants and their families at our local drug court program in Walker County and was asked to speak and be interviewed on WATC TV Live, Atlanta's community television. I had not searched for these opportunities, both great opportunities to share Hope with others fighting addiction came to me and asked for my story. Only God could take my story and our family's struggles and open doors that would lead me once again out of my comfort zone into His will to share my story, offer Hope, and let others know to pray with expectations as I had been told in 2011.

My husband said to me on our way home from the Atlanta Live television interview that our journey took a lot longer than it should have if we had just let go sooner. I said maybe, but God used every opportunity to get us ready for what was next. If our son was healed in Month 1 or Year 2 or anytime any sooner, then we would have missed the trials and tribulations that led us to our knowledge of addiction and our relationship with God that we now have. I would not have learned to surrender and truly trust God with my life and the life of my children. That surrender did not happen overnight or even over a few years. It is always easy to say what you should have done in hindsight, but we don't live each moment with that ability.

So, I take my journey along these last nine years and share with others so that if someone can see what we experienced, they will have a better understanding and know they are not alone. I hope to share these last nine years of being scattered, smothered, and yet totally covered by the grace of God throughout this book. I will share the stories, books read, words of encouragement given, and the good, bad, and ugly because truth is the only way I know how to share and to give hope in a hopeless situation.

CHAPTER 10

YEAR 2019

"Do not conform to the ways of the world but be transformed by the renewing of your mind. Then you will be able to test and approve what God's will is, His good, pleasing, and perfect will". Romans 12:2

2019 Holds a story all its own with so many lessons to learn.
Lesson 1
But God?
And Now What?

I was on Week 16 of a sixteen-week training plan with five training days left to go. It was May 13, 2019, and it would be my 2nd Half IRONMAN.

I see so many race reports comments about what was expected and how it turned out, but the real story is in the journey to the big day! On the "big day," you will either reach your goals or you will not, but what happens leading up to that time is the real goal and where the story is gathered. Little did I know what was soon to come.

What is this about?

How will I do this?

Where do I feel this is taking me?

But mostly for me, this time is… Why do I feel the need to do this?

Is this training and goal for me or for God's glory? If it is for me, it has been a difficult journey with little to no rewards except struggling, sinus infections, tight hamstrings, and aching and tight IT bands. This training has caused pain and frustration, along with loss of freedom to go and do as I would like. If it is for me, then this will be the last, if I even make it to the start line.

If this is for God and His Glory, then I want to push on through and see what He does on race day! At this point in my training, it will only be through God's power and strength that I start and finish as I should.

Since after race day last year, I have struggled with the direction God is leading. Does God want me to do another 70.3 or was that a one-time thing? God has not made it all clear to me, or have I ignored what He was telling me? At one point, I wrote "God says not now." Then later, I signed up, feeling as if I should.

Also, after last year's event, I went for my first post run, and the song that started playing was "Surrender" by Third Day. I remember even thinking, Why, God, would you have me hear so clearly a song that says surrender, stop running? But then I smiled to myself because after what He worked me into, He would never want me to stop, so I thought.

Surrender, by Third Day, lyrics

When the day began
And you opened your eyes
No, you didn't recognize
What you were seeing
Then it all came back
You remembered where you've been
Well, it never seems to end
And you're still running
Will you ever change your mind
You're almost out of time
You better give up
Gotta stop running

I should have paid more attention to that since that is how God spoke to me all throughout my training. Why would this be any different?

More of the lyrics that I heard and even wondered about yet put in the back of my head until it was almost too late.

Will you ever change your mind
You're almost out of time
You better give up Gotta stop running
It's the end of the line
It's time to surrender
Hands up Turn it around
Fall to the ground
Are you gonna surrender

What do we do when we search for the answer but cannot distinguish between our inner desires and God's desires?

It was so easy last year, 2018, to see where He wanted me to be and to train, learn, and share. This year has been so blurry in distinguishing His will versus my will.

So, what do I do? I will turn to His Word and search my heart. I will pray for eyes to see and ears to hear what the Lord has for me.

And I did, but I still wanted my way. I wanted that one more time to race and do it differently than last year. I had knowledge that I did not have last year. I knew what to expect, and I wanted to do it, even if everything was telling me not to.

That was not a good idea! It was a big mistake that could have cost me my life.

Okay, so I did not do too well at what I planned to do. Instead, I knew in my heart what He desired which was "not now", but I kept wanting to see if He had a last-minute change of heart.

This is Not advised!

For simplicity's sake, I will just say that in preparing for my last days prior to race day, one day after writing the start of this book, I almost went into cardiac arrest and/or stroke. I was doing cryotherapy which I had done pre-race and post-race last year with no problems. This year would not be the same. It sent me into extreme high blood pressure, an exploding headache, and vomiting profusely for forty-five-plus minutes until a 911 call and an ambulance came and took me to the emergency room. I am not exaggerating when I say I was begging God for mercy. I was begging for mercy and forgiveness because deep down I knew He had been saying "not now", but I was continually pushing against His will. Have you heard about Jonah and the fish? Well, that was me. I could have jumped into the Tennessee River and ended up in a catfish which was most likely what I deserved, but I did find myself in a hospital.

I may never know what went wrong in cryotherapy that evening, but I do know God stopped me in my tracks. Did He know I had a hidden condition that could be fatal if I participated? Was there a malfunction in the cryotherapy chamber, or was this His way of saying "I said no, not now"?

Have you found yourself, at times, pushing against God's will and felt the consequences whether mild or harsh? Remember, obedience is always better.

I had many tests done, and they are ruling out any hidden heart conditions and other possibilities that could have caused this. I prayed that I would get answers, especially pertaining to my health, but the most important lesson I learned is when He is speaking about a situation, be alert and obedient. What seems like no big deal could turn into a big deal with huge consequences.

As I wrote in one of my journals, "I am fairly certain that given a cape and a nice tiara, I could save the world." This is where my troubles began. I was certain, until my blood pressure went out of control, and my heart rate kept soaring. And. And. And.

Lesson 1

If only life was that easy and if only, I had listened and followed what I was being told. God speaks that voice if we only stop and listen. If you are faced with a challenge or desire, pause, pray, and seek God's direction. His desires for you are always better than our own.

Lesson 2

Discerning the Voice of God

Not everything God leads us through at one point should be repeated.

God led me to and through Ironman 70.3 Chattanooga in 2018, but in 2019, I kept hearing and sensing "No, not now." I sensed it but did not really think that He would not want me to. Maybe it was Satan trying to confuse me, or maybe I was not "discerning the voice of God" like I had studied earlier in the year.

We have a group of women that do Bible studies together. We call ourselves the Sister Stretch Team. We studied Discerning the Voice of God, how to recognize when God is speaking by Priscilla Shirer. I loved the study and took it to heart, I thought! I did love the study, but I must not have believed it mattered so much, or my actions would have been much different.

In chapter 3 of Discerning the Voice of God, I am looking back with hindsight, and the chapter is "What Do You Want?" and the scripture is "God is working in you, giving you the desire and the power to do what pleases Him" (Philippians 2:13 NLT). I had written just under that during our study, "Did that just give me confirmation to my last challenge?" I was writing about IRONMAN this year.

There is a key word that I missed... God is working in me to give me the desire and power to do what pleases Him, not me! "Pleases Him" is the key. He was not giving me the power to do IRONMAN so that I would be pleased. He wanted me to do what pleases Him, and He had been giving me the "No, not now" on IRONMAN most of the year.

Not all things are the right things and timing, even when it is not a bad thing. Keeping in shape and being healthy are desired by God. Our bodies are His temple. The spiritual, mental, and physical writings in the Daniel Plan help us refocus ourselves to live spiritually, physically, and mentally clean, but God can also speak to us in areas we may be overdoing or just not where He wants us to be at a time. Maybe, just maybe, He saw an idol forming.

In my first book, Endurance Race of Life and Addiction, God showed up and repeatedly directed my path of training, writing, and recognizing the voice of God. I had no doubt God was leading the way, His way for me to race the endurance race of life.

Then life goes on; I do a few different races to kick off the year. In January through April, I participated in 5Ks, 10Ks, 13.1 races to start preparing myself for what is to come, the 2019 IRONMAN 70.3. However, this year, it was more about what I wanted to do, and I ignored all the messages and discernment of His desires and did what I wanted. I was totally disobedient to His will and tried to justify why He would want me to participate. I wrestled with God for months, and I even processed at some point of how the disobedience in a physical activity equals a sinful act. How can something good for you not be good?

In one way, I knew God said not now, but in my flesh, I thought maybe I was not hearing Him clearly. Maybe it was just Satan messing with me. Bottom line, I wanted to do it. I must now ask myself why.

Why did I want it so badly? It is not like wanting a vacation with time to relax and rest. It is hard work and takes a considerable amount of time and energy to prepare for this type of event. Even when I took a vacation during the training time, I had to first work in my training schedule and find a place to run and swim. It takes great effort to participate in this type of endurance race. I believe most people do not desire this extreme activity. I know most people do not struggle with this desire, so why me and why now?

Why did I fight for my desire to do IRONMAN again this year instead of slowing down, relaxing, reading, camping and just being?

I get energized when I discuss the idea of doing it and when I see and talk to other athletes about it. It is what I will call a flesh thing. I believe the real reason God said No to this is because it is the one desire my flesh has that takes over other things. I am blessed in many ways that I can do it, but this activity takes a lot of time and effort. And I am not a spring chicken anymore!

Romans 8:9–13

"9. You, however, are not in the realm of the flesh but are in the realm of the Spirit, if indeed the Spirit of God lives in you. And if anyone does not have the Spirit of Christ, they do not belong to Christ. 10. But if Christ is in you, then even though your body is subject to death because of sin, the Spirit gives life because of righteousness. 11. And if the Spirit of him who raised Jesus from the dead is living in you, he who raised Christ from the dead will also give life to your mortal bodies because of his Spirit who lives in you. 12. Therefore, brothers and sisters, we have an obligation—but it is not to the flesh, to live according to it. 13. For if you live according to the flesh, you will die; but if by the Spirit you put to death the misdeeds of the body, you will live. Romans 8:9–13

Reread Romans 8:12–13 because that is exactly what almost happened to me, literally as I highlighted, you will die.

And then God shows me in the morning devotional Jesus Always, "My grace is sufficient for you. So, do not waste energy regretting how weak you feel, instead, embrace your insufficiency rejoicing how much you need Me. My power is made perfect in weakness."

Once again, I needed to be weakened before I could recognize Him or His will for me. **A strong determined mindset used without God's provisions and directions can be a dangerous thing.**

I need to focus on seeking to align myself with His will and make myself a living sacrifice as Sarah Young wrote in the devotional today. It will make my life meaningful and joyful, and isn't that what we are all searching and striving for?

Maybe that is the answer to my own questions of what makes the IRONMAN event so important to me. Why do I want it so badly? Why me, why now?

Because in writing and listening to God, it is becoming clearer that what I want, what we want, is something meaningful and joyful to exist in us.

The IRONMAN event is more meaningful to me than a 5K, 10K…because it requires so much more of me. It requires more structure, training, discipline, and willpower, and knowing I have worked on the training plans and completed this type of race brings accomplishment and joy.

Can I find meaning and joy in God's will versus my own will?

Absolutely, but I must surrender or die to self, and then God will use me. Words that I know and say but do not use often enough are surrender, humility, serve, trust, let go, stop, listen, breathe. All these should be first on my list of to-dos, but instead, I fill my to-do list with so many other tasks and goals that I miss the real goal of where and what I should set my mind on.

I have known all year that I was to start writing. I did not know what exactly but have had my writing area organized since the beginning of the year. But guess what I found out? It does not matter how organized you are if you never take the time to slow down, sit down, and write. God took care of that detail when I did not heed His warnings or will.

What I would not do, He did for me. God had been showing me for months to slow down and listen. He had different plans for me than what I had in mind. I was just going to put Him off just a bit until I finished my training and my upcoming 70.3!

What happened next was life-threatening but at the same time maybe lifesaving with lots of consequences to follow.

James 1:22-25

"Do not merely listen to the word, and so deceive yourselves. Do what it says. Anyone who listens to the word but does not do what it says is like someone who looks at his face in a mirror and, after looking at himself, goes away and immediately forgets what he looks like. But whoever looks intently into the perfect law that gives freedom and continues in it—not forgetting what they have heard but doing it—they will be blessed in what they do. James 1:22–25

Lesson 3

Hindsight Is 20/20

Were all the warnings and feelings I had about participating this year trying to protect me from something I did not know? Was the cryotherapy the disobedience I had progressed to that almost killed me, or was its God's last opportunity to stop me in my path before something fatal happened on the 70.3? Whichever the case may be, and I may never know for sure, the disobedience led to consequences that led to hospital visits by ambulance that night.

Hindsight Is Really 20/20

While in the emergency room from stroke-level blood pressure causing my head to feel as if it would explode off my head, extreme vomiting, and fear that I was going to die, I prayed for mercy over and over, asking God's forgiveness in repentance. I knew I had stepped across that line, and all I could do was pray for mercy and forgiveness.

It would have been so much better, easier, and healthier to do it His way to begin with. But I am thankful to say, He did show mercy and grace and allowed me to see some of the things He was trying to show me or protect me from.

We are to be content in our seasons, but for me, changing seasons is not easy to recognize. My MO is to go, move, do, work, go, go, go, go, go, and then something must happen to me to put the brakes on me.

Deep down, I knew I was feeling Him stirring my heart to stop, but I kept wanting it to be after the race, so I pushed on.

Could I have stopped the serious medical emergency that happened to me this week if I had heeded His warnings? Absolutely! But He also can take our mess ups and turn it into something good or lifesaving.

This time, God used it to get me back on track for His plan, not mine! We may deviate from God's plan, but He finds a way to get us back on track. This makes me think of the verse, Proverbs 16:9, In their heart's humans plan their course, but the Lord establishes their steps.

After another stroke-level blood pressure event landed me back in the hospital for three days and an abundance of testing, scans, and doctors, I am hoping to be closer to a diagnosis. Until we have all the answers to what is happening inside my body, the doctors have put me on rest, relaxation, and no exercise! Go figure; all this makes me sit down, get my writing in order, and start writing!

He got His way, but I had to deal with lots of dangerous consequences before getting to that!

God set the stage for me to write again, to start back where I left off. Here I am on scheduled medical rest, waiting for more testing and time for writing!

God is good; however, obedience is always easier than repentance. If you sense you are being disobedient to His will… Stop, back up, and do it His way! Do not wrestle God! His power is unlimited, and He sees what we cannot. Trust in Him and His goodness.

Lesson 4

When God Gives You Signs

When we recognize the signs or messages God is sending us, we need to make a note of them. Do not ignore or assume you did not really feel it, sense it, or hear it. Deep down, if you are one of those that feels the presence of God, and He has shown you something in the past, there is no reason to think He will not do it again.

This entire year prior to my emergency hospital visit, I felt like God was saying, "Not now, rest and restore, sit in my presence, and read and soak up my Word, don't go, do or travel..."

Now in my heart, I felt these things, but in my flesh, I wanted to believe that could not be. God created me to be busy, full of energy, and gave me motivation to go, do, and accomplish, so why would He be placing this on my heart? Well, He was, for a reason that I am still trying to find out.

I had been telling my husband that my chest felt pressure, my legs kept shooting pains in them and lots of cramps at night. I was having terrible IT band problems and other tight muscle aches, sinus infections repeatedly, and the list could go on. My point with this is that I ignored all the internal soul and external physical issues for one thing only...to do the IRONMAN 70.3. That is pretty "fleshy" and could have cost me my life. What do you give priority to that you know could harm you?

I had made comments and posts during my training schedule about wishing I could be content with camping, relaxing, and reading. I even said when things were busy, that I would love to have time to do nothing but read, study God's Word, rest, and relax. I started my year off this year with the word restoration. Every year, I decide what my word of the year is that will be my focus, and this year was to restore which should have told me it had nothing to do with pushing myself to do all things.

I was finally relieved from the burden of our son's eight-year addiction, which is a tremendous blessing. I wrote about my story of his addiction in Endurance Race of Life and Addiction in 2018, prior to knowing that he would be healed and saved from addiction. If you have ever dealt with anyone in addiction, it is harder than hard, so this was the year to restore what we lost in the previous eight hard years.

We bought a camper at the end of 2018, and it is a reflection, so my thoughts were to take trips, reflect, and restore. I even took that same theme into my office, and when everyone was to create their word for the year, I kept my work word as restoration as well.

Definition of restoration:

1. an act of restoring or the condition of being restored: such as a bringing back to a former position or condition:

Reinstatement the restoration of peace Instead of…

Definition of endurance:

1. the ability to withstand hardship or adversity especially the ability to sustain a prolonged stressful effort or activity a marathon runner's endurance

2. the act or an instance of enduring or suffering endurance of many hardships

3. Permanence, Duration
   the endurance of the play's importance

Okay, the definition that I chose when I chose the word restoration for 2019 doesn't look at all what I set hard and fast to do by challenging myself to the fullest in an endurance race like an IRONMAN event. I stated, "restoration", but I acted on "endurance".

In hindsight, God was saying No to IRONMAN, No to Training, flat out No to my desires. And yet I trained, traveled, and planned future race events, which landed me in a bad place. I had to cancel reservations I had made for travel and biking trips that cost me loss of deposits and loss of wasted time put into all of them. What is God telling you? What do you need to stop before God stops you?

It still amazes me that the more I recognized these signs, the more I put them aside because it did not match my plan. I tried to justify my plan with "what could it hurt if I did an endurance race?" It is active and healthy, but only if you do not have a hidden medical condition or God is saying No.

So here I am, I dreamed of having time to do nothing but read, study God's word, rest, and relax. I just did not think it would happen any time soon or especially now. I sit now from doctor's orders, with my dream fulfilled of doing nothing, and that feels overwhelming. Change always is even if it is a positive change.

I also did not imagine what it would truly look like. It is one thing to say you want to go away, read, and do nothing until that is all you can do. I have had to figure out what resting and doing nothing is to look like. It is the same with healing. We may want to be healed, but it can be overwhelming while making the necessary changes to be healed.

We always want what we do not have, until we have it. The grass is always greener on the other side, until we are on the other side and realize our grass was green right where we were!

So, for whatever reason, God saw fit to set me down, and so here I sit in front of my computer doing what He most likely intended me to do to begin with. I would have preferred to sit down without health issues, but God knows that would probably not happen. It Wasn't Happening.

In reading one of my daily devotionals, Mary Southerland wrote in Girlfriends in God on June 6, "Living for Jesus… Today!" In it she says, "No doubt about it. Life is short. And this brief life is nothing more than a dress rehearsal for eternity. Every minute of every day is either **spent** or **invested**".

What makes the difference?

1. Purpose

2. Resting in God while wholeheartedly pursuing God's plan.

3. Surrendering every part of every day to Him, knowing that nothing touches our lives without passing through His hands—with His permission.

4. Those interruptions we complain about may very well be God-ordained opportunities through which His grace, love and forgiveness are poured.

We need to live each day with the mindset that we are God with skin on. Our heart desire should be for God to use us to accomplish His plan and purpose in the lives in each person we meet.

And then there is this quote from Denzel Washington:

"At the end of the day, it's not about what you have or even what you've accomplished. It is about who you lifted, who you have made better. It's about what you have given back.

Lesson 5

Fight or Flight

I am not a fighter. Never have been and never will be. In real danger, I kick into flight mode. When I have big disappointments, I run off and get out of town—flight!

I was taught not to say foul language. In the south, we can't say cuss words, but some spell them out. I am not sure if that is universal, but if we spell it in the south, that makes it seem okay!

The first evidence for me of fight or flight is when my Mom said a cuss word, and she did not spell it; she said it loud and clear.

I was about twelve years old when I heard her say her first cuss word. I could not believe she could do such a thing. I mean, she was a real Christian and never cussed or yelled…so when my Mom said this cuss word, it was time for me to hit the road. I ran away which, in later years, I realized is my MO in tough times.

I prepared, as I also realize is my MO, by packing saltine crackers and getting my dad's thermal coat because I didn't know where this journey would lead, but I wanted to make sure I would be warm and well-fed. I also got all the money I had, which was about $13 to cover any cost.

I walked about a mile and saw some of my friends playing football in their front yard. I joined them for a little bit without telling them my plan. I was not quite sure I knew it yet. Then I headed downtown where I knew my previous babysitter lived and showed up at her house.

I told her the story of how it was time for me to go. I asked her to get me a taxi. I am not sure why she did, but she did, and the taxi driver was at her house shortly after and I got in.

Now I could be telling a horrible story of what happened in that taxi, but fortunately, it was not a bad ride. I sat in the back seat and leaned on the front seat and talked to the driver all the way down to the next town twenty minutes away. I directed him to a family friend's house while pointing the way. I had no idea of an address. I just knew their names and where they lived.

I did not have enough money with the $13 to pay the taxi driver, so now my parents' friends had me at their door ready to move in as soon as they could pay my taxi fare. I am thankful they loved me all the way through this.

I tell you this to say even as a young girl, instead of fighting about it, I set into organizing and planning mode and hit the road. It was the first time I did this, but it would not be the last that I took flight over fight. But some things in time must change. I may be starting to learn how to fight since flight will not always be an option.

Just for information's sake, the family said I could stay with them for as long as I wanted, but they had to let my parents know, and they did. Shortly after that call, my dad was there to pick me up, worried and upset that I had done that. I do think my mom cussed at least two times since that event over forty-four years ago, and once I had my own kids, that made more sense. She is still a "saint" in my mind. If I only caused her to do it once in my raising, she is evidently a woman of faith, love, and a lot of patience.

I wanted to share that story so you can see my MO on fight or flight and to also try to get you to recognize your MO in times of stress, disappointments, or difficult circumstances.

With my newest health issues, I will need to learn to fight, not flight. I will not be able to outrun it, leave town and get far away from it, or even—or especially—exercise my way out of it. I will have to face it, fight it, and do it with the trust in God and the trust in all my physicians along the way. I cannot pack my bags, organize my supplies, and head out anywhere to make it go away. So, I will pray about it, trust God in it, and hopefully I will be able to glorify Him in and through it.

When we are in flight mode, our adrenaline kicks into high gear, and with what appears to be my possible diagnosis, I cannot let my adrenaline kick in, or it can kick me out!

In 2019, I was still waiting for a full diagnosis, but with tumors on both my adrenal glands, I couldn't take a chance with getting stressed, excited, or physically asserted by exercise… I can do **Nothing** because it sends my blood pressure to stroke level very quickly. I have overcome two episodes, but the doctor says the third one may not be a charm, so I must listen and obey right now. I wish I had done that the first time with God. Maybe then, I would not be in this spot now.

We never know if we will get one more try, chance or episode especially when dealing with drugs. Don't wait.

I Will Fight This Time

- Fight against what is my normal MO of flight

- Fight to do what is necessary instead of what I want to do

- Fight to let others do what I cannot do

- Fight to share my workload and give up control

- Fight against the desire to exercise until I know more

- Fight this battle and anything Satan tries to deceive me with

- Fight not to get caught up in the unknown

- Fight like a girl that knows how to fight

I am recognizing it is time for "less of me and more of Thee." So, I will fight my normal actions and reactions and let the desires of my heart relate to God's will in this life event for such a time as these.

While I was writing this part one evening, a dear sweet lady sent me a message through messenger with this poem.

One Day at a Time

One day at a time, with its failures and fears,
With its hurts and mistakes, with its weakness and tears,
With its portion of pain and its burden of care.
One day at a time we must meet and must bear.
One day at a time to be patient and strong,
To be calm under trial and sweet under wrong.
Then its toiling shall pass, and its sorrow shall cease.
It shall darken and die, and the night shall bring peace.
One day at a time—but the day is so long,
And the heart is not brave, and the soul is not strong,

O Thou pitiful Christ, be Thou near all the way.
Give courage and patience and strength for the day.
Swift cometh His answer, so clear and so sweet.
"Yea, I will be with thee, thy troubles to meet.
I will not forget thee, nor fail thee, nor grieve.
I will not forsake thee; I never will leave."
Not yesterday's load we are called on to bear,
Nor the morrow's uncertain and shadowy care.
Why should we look forward or back with dismay?
Our needs, as our mercies, are but for the day.
One day at a time, and the day is His day.
He hath numbered its hours, though they haste or delay.
His grace is sufficient; we walk not alone.
As the day, so the strength that He giveth His own
By, Annie Johnson Flint, given to me by Sarah Jones

Lesson 6

God Provides

Does anyone else read devotionals daily?

If not, I highly recommend it. That is something you can do in the morning, afternoon, or evening, and God speaks to you at that time just where you are. It always amazing me how I read right what I need to read at that very moment I need it.

I love the Jesus Calling versions by Sarah Young. I have been reading the Jesus Always most recently. It never fails which version I read on what day; it is right where I am whether joyful, struggling, sick, hurting, running… He places before me just what I need. He meets me where I am, always.

Whatever way I choose that day to connect spiritually, whether in reading His Word, a devotional, or in music, He provides what I need just at the right time.

He really is our daily bread, providing spiritual nourishment only at the time of need, our daily manna. He does not overload us with it so that some of it is wasted or thrown out. He gives just as much as we need or can handle for that day.

This makes me think of the Lord's Prayer in Luke 11 (NIV).

Jesus's Teaching on Prayer

One day Jesus was praying in a certain place. When he finished, one of his disciples said to him, "Lord, teach us to pray, just as John taught his disciples."

He said to them, "When you pray, say:

'Father, hallowed be your name, your kingdom come.

Give us each day our daily bread.

Forgive us our sins, for we also forgive everyone who sins against us.

And lead us not into temptation.'"

God gives us just enough—just enough direction, just enough daily bread so that none is wasted.

Lesson 7

Grace—God Gives and God Takes Away

On May 12, Mother's Day, a stray puppy came to our house. I felt from that first day that God placed her with us. It was love at first sight, and I named her Grace. She filled a space in my heart that wanted to give love. I wanted to hold her much more than an active puppy wanted to be held. She was sweet, playful, and loved our other two big dogs tremendously. She loved, and we loved her back.

And then, exactly thirty days later and almost to the hour, Grace died. We do not know exactly what happened to her, but the vet said she had a large mass on her lungs which was very unusual. Maybe the booster shot she got the day before caused this or the combination of the two. We most likely will never know, but it is so much my same story that is evolving. I too seemed and looked healthy and happy, but an unknown tumor on my lungs and adrenal glands kicked a reaction into motion that almost killed me.

My husband and I were devastated and are still feeling such heartache. We both sobbed and then sobbed some more. My heart was broken, and my emotions were a wreck which caused my blood pressure to start rising.

How does something this small in such a short period of time make such an impact on us? Is this God preparing us little by little on what to expect? Is He teaching us in smaller doses how to handle grief, so we better handle it with harder grief issues?

Why Grace and why now, Lord? I prayed for Grace this morning. My prayer was...what do I take from this, and what do I write? I know you gave me Grace, but I do not know why you took her.

My heart and soul will remember that sweet Grace and the joy she brought in thirty days here and the sadness we felt the day she was gone.

Lord, comfort us when we cannot comfort ourselves.

For a time, such as this…

Was Grace the "sacrificial Lamb" as in the dictionary, "sacrificed for the common good," "supporting character whose sole purpose is to die"?

I have said, if these things must happen to write a chapter, I may not want to write any more. I keep thinking of "God gave me a thirty-day Grace period," but why and for what?

This same day is the day that I saw the pulmonologist for the first time about the tumor or nodule they found on my lung. Is there a connection or just a time to open the floodgates of emotion of what we have been going through for almost thirty days with my health issues and findings.

Was this even harder because we both faced some tough realities through Grace? My heart still aches for her and will continue to ache. She made a huge impact on us and our other four-legged ones in such a short time with such sweet demeanor and yet feisty and fearless!

And then,…the only other thing I can say about today is, "only when it is quiet."

Lesson 8

Only When It Is Quiet

If we keep busy enough, we don't have the need to sit and be still, to be quiet, but when we have something happen in our lives, like a death an illness or hurt of any kind, it takes the wind out of us and leaves us sitting. In my case, also by doctors' orders. Even though the doctors told me to do nothing, I was still doing some things around the house which meant I still was not totally sitting in God's presence, being still and listening. I was making sure some business got taken care of, bills paid, emails sent, yada, yada, yada.

Then today, my husband and I both lost it. We could not talk; we did not know why this was happening…and then the downloads of questions came as if God was right there to hear me. I do not have the answers, but someday I may. What I do know, when we throw our arms up in the air and ask why, He may not give us the answers, but He will give us His presence.

His grace is sufficient, and His power is made perfect.

2 Corinthians 12:9 New International Version

9 But he said to me, "My grace is sufficient for you, for my power is made perfect in weakness." Therefore, I will boast all the more gladly about my weaknesses, so that Christ's power may rest on me.

While sitting in the patient room at the pulmonologist's office, it came to me that most of the time we ask, "why me" when the question should be "why not me." Why should it be different or better for me? Why should I not have problems and others should or do? So, for today and hopefully throughout this process, the question will be why not me?

I am a child of God, I know and trust my God, and if me, then me. I should not be any different than any other soul out there struggling and suffering from what life throws at us. I have not earned a higher seat of no problem, hurt, or pain, and neither has anyone else. We just need to know what we know, trust the one that can be trusted, and know we are loved to the fullest.

Through this entire event, God has been there. He has provided just enough, given me just enough grace and mercy and provided our daily bread even if it was prepared and provided by our friends and relatives, just at the right time and just enough! I want to add; I am blessed to live in a small southern town where prayers are abundant and so is the food that is given by those closest to us during these times.

Just enough!

Lesson 9

Be Still and Know that I Am God

I heard the birds, saw the baby birds, made lemonade and mint water…we planted lavender and hung the porch swing. I read two books and started another one. I sat and visited with family and friends. I breathed, I saw, and I heard what I had not heard in a long time.

In Psalm 46:10, He says, "Be still, and know that I am God; I will be exalted among the nations, I will be exalted in the earth." And Exodus 14:14 says, "The Lord will fight for you; you need only to be still."

Why is it so hard to "be still" in God? When I do it, I see all the wonderful benefits that go along with it.

Psalm 46:1–11

God is our refuge and strength, an ever-present help in trouble. Therefore, we will not fear, though the earth gives way, and the mountains fall into the heart of the sea, though its waters roar and foam and the mountains quake with their surging. There is a river whose streams make glad the city of God, the holy place where the Most High dwells. God is within her; she will not fall; God will help her at break of day. Nations are in uproar, kingdoms fall; he lifts his voice, the earth melts. The Lord Almighty is with us; the God of Jacob is our fortress. Come and see what the Lord has done, the desolations he has brought on the earth. He makes wars cease to the ends of the earth. He breaks the bow and shatters the spear; he burns the shields with fire. He says, "Be still, and know that I am God; I will be exalted among the nations, I will be exalted in the earth." The Lord Almighty is with us; the God of Jacob is our fortress.

In the Moody Bible Commentary, it says Psalm 46:8–11 are for comfort and divine refuge. The psalmist closed this psalm with words of encouragement. It says that in the closing words of comfort, God also included a challenge to cease striving, relax, and know that I am God.

So, the "be still" doesn't mean just to literally sit down or sit still; it means even more. Besides sitting still, we are to stop striving.

I don't know about you, but just because I sit still doesn't mean I won't get a pad and pen and start writing my to-do list or work projects, check emails, and the list goes on. This is where God is saying, "Stop, Be Still, Stop Striving…and know that I am God. I got this, let Me do it, not your way but My way. You do not have to 'fix it.' Just sit, be still, and know that I am Your comfort and refuge now and for always."

So, I will take all this as be still, stop striving, and have eyes to see and eyes to hear what God gives me. I do not need to strive or work so hard to see and hear. God will provide at just the right time.

Just be still.

Definition of be

1. Exist synonyms: exist, have being, have existence; more

2. occur; take place. "the exhibition will be in November" synonyms: occur, happen, take place, come about, arise, crop up, transpire, fall, materialize, ensue.

I believe in this statement: God is saying "exist" is nothing more and nothing less, just exist.

Definition of still adjective

1. not moving or making a sound.

"the still body of the young man" synonyms: motionless, unmoving, without moving, without moving a muscle, stock-still, immobile, like a statue, as if turned to stone, as if rooted to the spot, unstirring, stationary.

noun

1. deep silence and calm; stillness. "the still of the night" synonyms: quietness, quiet, quietude, silence, stillness, hush, soundlessness, noiselessness; more

2. an ordinary static photograph as opposed to a motion picture, especially a single shot from a movie.

adverb

1. up to and including the present or the time mentioned; even now (or then) as formerly. "He still lives with his mother." synonyms: up to this time, up to the present time, until now, even now, yet "I understand he's still married to her."

synonyms:

nevertheless, however, in spite of that, despite that, notwithstanding, for all that, all the same, even so, be that as it may, having said that, nonetheless, but;

verb

1. make or become still; quieten. "She raised her hand, stilling Erica's protests."

    synonyms: quieten, quiet, silence, hush;

And as far as "still", I believe it is as the verb is shown, make or become still; quieten, quiet, silence, hush...

When we put those two together, we get "be still" or "just exist quietly." I have not been doing either of these much less both very well. But when I finally did, I could see and hear Him, feel His presence, and know He is not depending on me to get it done!

Now with that being said, I also realize the minute I stand up, my mind kicks into what to get done so I have to pause and process, is He done with me "being still", and if not, sit back down, and if He is, move on. It is a lifelong habit to be moving and doing, so this will take practice over and over before it becomes natural for me.

In 2020, it still does not come naturally, but with COVID-19, I am coming to that place out of requirements and necessity.

My morning devotional yesterday was about a good father and how when a father leads his four-year-old son down a crowded street, he takes him by the hand and says, "Hold on to me." He does not say, "Memorize the map" or "Take your chances dodging the traffic" or "Let us see if you can find your way home." The good father gives the child one responsibility: "Hold on to my hand."

It goes on to say, God does the same with us. Do not load yourself down with lists. Do not enhance your anxiety with the fear of not fulfilling it. Your goal is not to know every detail of the future. Your goal is to hold the hand of the One who does and never, ever let go.

And for the last twenty-four hours, I was still. And then God showed up and showed out!

Lesson 10

But God!

When I wrote earlier about the word for the year, our Bible study group, Sister Stretch or Real Sisters (Relationships, Encouragement, Accountability, and Laughter), decided we would name it Name Your Season. We had a mixture of words from all of us picking our word. I had chosen restoration. Other words that were chosen were peace, obedience, arise, cleanse, restoration, reflection, audacious, and…

Unity and Maturity in the Body of Christ

Ephesians 4:1-7

As a prisoner for the Lord, then, I urge you to live a life worthy of the calling you have received. Be completely humble and gentle; be patient, bearing with one another in love. Make every effort to keep the unity of the Spirit through the bond of peace. There is one body and one Spirit, just as you were called to one hope when you were called; one Lord, one faith, one baptism; one God and Father of all, who is over all and through all and in all. But to each one of us grace has been given as Christ apportioned it. This is why it says: "When he ascended on high, he took many captives and gave gifts to his people."

Before I ever started this book or thought of one, God placed before me the study Discerning the Voice Of God: How to Recognize When God Is Speaking by Priscilla Shirer as I now know as my beginning story bookend.

This is one of the first studies my Stretch, aka Real Sisters, took on. On the other side of this book is the other story bookend. He provided this as a suggestion from one of my dearest friends and Real Sisters while I was in the hospital called, "Life Interrupted": Navigating the Unexpected, also by Priscilla Shirer.

A few thoughts come to mind of how God used the same author as my story's bookends and what Priscilla Shirer would think if she knew a book she completely revised and expanded in 2012 would lead me into my journey, and the book she wrote in 2011 the previous year would be my ending bookmark. God knew what He was doing in Priscilla in 2011 and 2012 that I would need in 2019 that would be the bookends for my story and help me search my heart and motives.

What is so much more amazing to me is that God is God, and it is possible for Him to do amazingly more than anything I could imagine. Priscilla Shirer and other authors are so blessed and talented in their spiritual gifts of writing, but the real amazing thing to me is that through people like Priscilla Shirer and by God's hand and direction, He can use me. I am not a writer. I am not well versed in scripture or theology. I am a sinner who loves the Lord and wants to do His will, most of the time. I am a believer, worshipper, and yet still trying to get it right. What I do know is that no matter where we are, God meets us there, even if it is with some health issues, heartache, and/or major consequences. We cannot outrun our problems or desires, but thankfully, we cannot outrun God or the love of God either.

I wanted to compete one last time, but God wanted differently, and God is the only reason and way.

Not my way, but God's!

I highlighted, underlined, and made notes several places in the Discerning the Voice of God. I have included a few of these.

"Or have you already filled in every conceivable space with your own opinions, ideas, decisions, and actions—space that God might otherwise fill with His perfectly timed and previsions and personal insight?"

"Listen up… What's on your question plate right now is most likely an "either/or" kind of thing."

"Listening period is a lost art. We rarely listen to each other, much less the unseen God. Instead, we've inserted a lot of noise and activity".

"Have we become so addicted to busyness— not merely in our daily lives but while we're actually immersed in our daily devotions—that we've trained ourselves not to hear Him?"

"To hear Him, I must listen. Think. Concentrate on Him. Meditate."

And Chapter Challenges written out.

"Allow for and accept 'God margins' in all areas of your life. Relax instead of trying to fill every space with your own ideas, decisions, and actions." I even added my own here to remember He knows how to make it happen. I should add here, He does, but I did not follow along.

Priscilla says, "Close this book and take time now to think about what your 'gut' is telling you to do regarding a current decision you are facing."

I did and even wrote, "The book—when and how to finish,".

And then in chapter Three, "What Do You Want? God Is Working in You, Giving You the Desire and the Power to Do What Pleases Him,"

I wrote beside that, "Did that just give me confirmation to my last challenge?" I thought or wanted to think that God was saying yes to IRONMAN 70.3, 2019. However, I was ignoring the desires and comments I had written earlier about relaxing, restoring, resting, and doing His will. I thought, Just one more time for IRONMAN, and I can do better than last year in what I learned.

Wrong again! "Just one more time" is a comment that should send us a mental alert once we say it. Why one more time and what are the possible consequences from doing something "just one more time".

As I wrote earlier from the scripture she uses of Philippians 2:13 (NLT), "For God is working in you, giving you the desire and the power to do what pleases Him," God's work in you is to cause you to desire His will for your life—to align with His—then giving you the energy to carry out the plans He's mapped out for you to participate in. I was looking for Him to give me the energy to carry out the plans I had to race, not to align myself with His plan.

"Delight yourself in the Lord; and He will give you the desires of your heart" Psalm 37:4. I was working for Him to delight Himself in my desires. I was not letting Him transform me, but I was trying to transform Him, but God does not work that way!

Per Priscilla, "leave room for God to be God."

And then she writes, "And still today, He steadily, continually pursues His saints, even when they—even when we—are running hard in the opposite direction (which I was literally doing). He loves us, so He keeps it up. Never tires out. Never backs down, (even if it means placing our back ends in the hospital to get us to stop running and resisting).

She adds later, "Sometimes, in fact, His voice is clearest when we're in situations we don't prefer." I must agree totally because until God took me off my training path of IRONMAN, I did not have time to hear Him and accept His plan clearly. I was able to justify my desires even though I had underlined "He may open before you a season of rest, refreshment, and celebration." And I had added "hopeful."

He was giving me the heart's desire for this; I just would not listen, but God took care of that for me. I have had to rest and sit with little to no activity for six weeks now and still waiting for one more test result to come in.

I will say clearly and confidently now, no matter what the test results show or what I am released from or to do, I know that God has the plan for me, and it is to sit in His presence and do His will, not mine.

So, these are the things I had taken to heart, written on, or highlighted starting in the last few months of 2018. I studied the book and the Bible study together with my REAL Sisters and alone, but then I did what Jonah did…hence the bookend of my story.

While recently reading Life Interrupted by Priscilla Shirer, it became so evident to me that I had played the role of Jonah from start to finish. Priscilla starts off in chapter 1 with the verse "For since the world began, no ear has heard, and no eye has seen a God like you, who works for those who wait for him!" Isaiah 64:4 NLT. I highlighted "who wait for him!" Not me, not this time.

If only, like Priscilla, I wish I had known then what I know now! I did not even know when I started this book or even part of the way through that I resembled Jonah so much. I had not even thought of Jonah and his story when considering mine. I had been highlighting a few of the sentences

Priscilla wrote like "And yet God has let it happen anyway" and "I knew what it was like to watch circumstances maneuvering around me in such a way that God's hand was obviously on them, drawing me to come along, asking me to trust Him enough to cooperate with His purpose." and "Why do we still run from Him and His plans?"

At this point, I was thinking, I do not spiritually run, but I literally run for some reason. I even put a big asterisk by "I want my life to radiate what happens when God has a person's heart at His full control, when every event or circumstance is simply another avenue to know Him better and show forth His glory." Wow, I highlighted it and marked it as important, but still not realizing how this would start to speak to me and where my heart was fully heading until I read more.

She adds, "What if we knew this interrupted life was less about the problem and more about the process? What if we knew that the direction, He was taking us provided opportunities we'd always dreamed about, even if they didn't look exactly the way we thought they would?" At this point, I started realizing that what happened to me was not only a divine interruption from God, but it would bring me freedom I desired and physically needed without me even knowing I needed it until I had it.

I had dreamed of traveling around the country, relaxing, and restoring myself while studying the Word of God. I didn't know what the actual outcome from this event would lead to, but God would show me the way, and it would be just where I needed to be in the first place before I played the character of Jonah.

Between COVID-19, health issues, my ability and freedom to travel, 2020 has come to play, and I have had time to see, hear, and praise the Lord.

When I read, "The word of the Lord is designed to reshape your purposes, putting you in position for Him to do through you what you cannot do on your own." I knew this event or redirection was bigger than I could imagine. This is about the time I thought, I cannot wait to read what else she has to say. This is reaching me in a place I had not gone so deep as to look at.

On the surface, I knew it was all by God's direction, whether from my disobedience or His redirection, but I wasn't thinking and still don't know what to think about how big and how broad this event could redirect. However, it did set me back down to start writing again which is only possible through God.

"Yielding to His call…we always succeed when we surrender." I know that in my head, but this time, I am starting to understand it at a heart level as well. When we first surrender, we begin to see success soon to follow. Success can look like many different things so don't get hung up on "success".

I also find it God's desire for me to keep reading… Part 2 is "On the Run" which I have spent my life doing. I have written in this section, "running from what, who and why?" I know I am a runner in many aspects. I enjoy running and the challenge of it. I enjoy the escape from everyday life while doing it, but I also know as stated before, I run from stress. I have a flight mentality, not a fight mentality.

So, running is my MO.

Priscilla writes, "Our running is really a vain attempt to keep from having to deal with a holy God and His sovereign authority." And I added "or deal with something like the unknown." What are you running from and what do you run to as your coping mechanism? Watch out!

I was telling a couple of girlfriends at dinner about this time what happened with the medical emergency and why I knew it was God that stopped me in my tracks. I stated I was starting to write a book about "Obedience versus Repentance" and how I knew that I had been disobedient to the voice of God. I had tried to justify why God would be "okay" with me participating in the IRONMAN… I called it disobedience, and my girlfriend called it PRIDE. And that made me stop and think.

I had been very aware of someone else's pride issue that I am close to and even had been saying to watch out for pride. Pride comes before the fall.

But was what I had been doing prideful or what? What sin do I attach my situation to?

With that, I looked up the seven deadly sins. Here Is what I found.

Many people are asking, "What are the seven deadly sins?"

The seven deadly sins viewed by society and literature are:

1. Lust. To have an intense desire or need. "But I tell you that anyone who looks at a woman lustfully has already committed adultery with her in his heart" (Matthew 5:28).

2. Gluttony. Excess in eating and drinking. "For drunkards and gluttons become poor, and drowsiness clothes them in rags" (Proverbs 23:21).

3. Greed. Excessive or reprehensible acquisitiveness. "Having lost all sensitivity, they have given themselves over to sensuality so as to indulge in every kind of impurity, with a continual lust for more" (Ephesians 4:19).

4. Laziness. Disinclined to activity or exertion; not energetic or vigorous. "The way of the sluggard is blocked with thorns, but the path of the upright is a highway" (Proverbs 15:19).

5. Wrath. Strong vengeful anger or indignation. "A gentle answer turns away wrath, but a harsh word stirs up anger" (Proverbs 15:1).

6. Envy. Painful or resentful awareness of an advantage enjoyed by another joined with a desire to possess the same advantage. "Therefore, rid yourselves of all malice and all deceit, hypocrisy, envy, and slander of every kind. Like newborn babies, crave pure spiritual milk, so that by it you may grow up in your salvation" (1 Peter 2:1–2).

7. Pride. Quality or state of being proud—inordinate self-esteem. "Pride goes before destruction, a haughty spirit before a fall" (Proverbs 16:18).

I studied these and even talked to my friend about these seven deadly sins, and which had I done. As I study them again, I see several that could apply. I was lustful for my desires of accomplishment and for the high that type of event puts me in. I was a glutton for exercise in an excessive way. Not that exercise is bad, but when it became excessive to what God's plans were for me, and I would not stop, it became a gluttony of exercise or gluttony of getting my way. I could include greed as in the greed of continual lust for more. I find it hard to see laziness in this except for lazy in doing God's will because mine seemed more fun. I do not see any wrath in my choices, but I can tell you I sure felt God's wrath in it. And as far as envy, I envied all the other athletes I read about and watched prepare, train, and complete their goals.

Of the seven deadly sins, I could have contributed to any or all of six out of seven, and I experienced the other one, the "wrath" from God. I encourage you to watch your choices and whether you are being obedient to God, or if by your choices, you are allowing any of these sins to cause disobedience. Obedience is much easier and more rewarding than repentance and redirection by God.

And to add to the "running" theme, Priscilla adds, "No where's far enough, and no price is too steep when you're running from God. But in running—even if it is the inside, unseen kind—we place ourselves in the worst possible position we could be in. We stand outside of God's will, outside of His blessings."

I was seeing firsthand the truth in this. My friend couldn't have recommended a better book for me during this time, or should I say, God couldn't have placed a better book in the heart of my friend to share with me during this time to help me see clearly or discern better the will of God, which was to "stop running for a while and start following His plan."

Now do not misunderstand me when I say He wants me to stop running. I do know He wants me to stop for now, but I do not believe that will always be the case. I think He needed me to stop running long enough to redirect my path. I was filling up my days with the same work, family, friends, exercise which did not allow any time for redirection to happen naturally.

I could go on and on with quotes from Priscilla's writings in Life Interrupted based on the highlights and notes I wrote while reading it, but what I needed to hear from God may not be the same for you.

I know without a doubt that God wanted me to hear and relate to Jonah as the one running from His calling or duty while God had asked him to do something he did not want to do.

Was it any one or all the seven deadly sins or some other sin that kept Jonah to do what God wanted him to do? We may not have all the answers, but it is clear when God redirected Jonah and myself, He stopped us right where we were and placed us in a whale and a hospital to stop our running. At that point, He had our attention, and we were at that point—and only that point—where we were willing to look at what God was desiring.

I desire to have eyes to see and ears to hear.

"Whoever has ears, let them hear." Matthew 13: 9

I do not want to fall into this again.

Ezekiel 12:2 NKJV

"Son of man, you dwell in the midst of a rebellious house, which has eyes to see but does not see, and ears to hear but does not hear; for they are a rebellious house." Ezekiel 12:2 NKJV

I want to get it right this time! I want to remember where I was and remember why I do not want to return to that which was my way, not God's way.

I do want to add one more Priscilla quote that she wrote toward the end of her book. "Doesn't it stand to reason that our enemy—the all-star running coach—would want us out on the track every second if something eternally spectacular might arise from our going God's way instead?"

I thank God for using Priscilla over eight years ago to sit and write the book Life Interrupted for such a time as this for me and that God spoke through her in terms of running and running coaches that would touch my heart and grasp my understanding.

And then, But God! My husband and I went to the doctor's appointment where we were to find out what was next. It wasn't going to be good…the plans for Emory or Vanderbilt, what we thought would be the next few months of procedures, test, surgeries, and more surgery, But God—but God changed that.

That is not a but God? But a "but God!" could do it!

The last two hospital stays, doctors, CT scans, and MRIs said one thing, but God said differently. I was told the next week that I did not have pheochromocytoma as they had thought, and I would not be going to Vanderbilt or Emory and there would be no surgeries at this point. I would just be scanned regularly and reviewed. Amazing! I should have been saying since the beginning of this year, "I want to swim, bike, run, and do another 70.3 again, But God sees differently this year."

When there is a "but God," we need to pay attention. We need to be willing to die to selfish desires and follow God's desires. We do not know what our future holds or where He wants us always, but God does. God could have walked away from me when I was ignoring Him, but He chased me, He fought for me, and then He provided for me throughout.

I heard this song again, and today it meant so much more because of the way He has touched me recently. "God has been so good to me. He chases me down, fights 'til I am found, the never-ending reckless love of God!"

BOOKEND THEME SONGS

Reckless Love (Song by Cory Asbury)

Before I spoke a word, You were singing over me
You have been so, so good to me
Before I took a breath, You breathed Your life in me
You have been so, so kind to me
Oh, the overwhelming, never-ending, reckless love of God

I don't deserve it, still You give Yourself away.
Oh, the overwhelming, never-ending, reckless love of God, yeah.
Source: LyricFind Songwriters: Caleb Culver, Cory Asbury, Ran Jackson

Ending theme song in 2019:
Alive, by Big Daddy Weave

I was dead in my transgressions
Wandering in sin
I went searching for redemption
Down a road that had no end
I was walking through this fire
I was living on the run
With my flesh lost in desire
I was drowning in the flood
But God
Rich in mercy
You came to save me
Now I'm alive

I said, "But God?
God said, But God!

Thoughts to Process written down.

What fills you up or what consumes you?

If what consumes you does not fill you with joy and peace of the Spirit, then maybe you are consuming the wrong things, even if those things are good. Food, exercise, church projects and events, family and friends are examples of good things, but not our number one priority. Seeking and loving God first is of upmost importance. We were created to glorify God, not ourselves.

Psalm 51:10

Create in me a pure heart, O God, and renew a steadfast spirit in me.

On March 12, 2019, I wrote, As much natural beauty God created on this trip, the only time I hear Him is when I emerge or submerge myself in a quiet run with ear plugs in or swim with face down in the water to drown out all the outside noise and entertainment. It is in this time alone in the quietness of the water, a run, or a bike ride that I hear Him most clearly. There is so much beauty to see in our travels that it can be overstimulating. This requires intentional stopping to reflect, rest, and restore.

If you want to know God's desires and will for your life, you must pause long enough to hear Him. I will add, especially on vacation where we want to do it all in a limited number of days. In the excitement and rush, it is easy to forget to stop, thank the One that created this beauty and the availability to travel and experience it and to thank Him for His blessings.

I ended with, "I choose to pause, reflect, and restore before going back into life's routine door." That may be the last time I paused before the 911 emergency room event in May.

We need to reflect light in this world, not a flash of light living in our own flesh. We were created to love others as ourselves and minister to others, but if we are too caught up in our own stuff, we don't have time or energy to be the light for others.

At the beginning of the year, I wrote, "A day of revelation—need time to reflect, restore, and reset. The year of R's—Renew, Restart, Reflect, Restore, Reset, Remember, Realize, and Recognize."

I realized getting into God's Word every morning had become a task or a "to do" on my mental list that I checked off. I do not ever want it to be a task or a job but a privilege and a blessing. I want to remember that I get to; I do not have to.

It is time to reflect on how to hear God's voice and to sit in His presence, my timeline, and how and where I see and hear God.

I will begin new, renewed, and ready if only now that He has my attention!

And now I will start the writing you gave me the title of ten years ago, and I pray that I will hear and see you all the way through this process and that when I hear you, I choose obedience over disobedience because even partial disobedience is still disobedience.

I want more!

The following are quotes from Anthony Carter in Running from Mercy, which hit home with me:

"We rationalize our disobedience and our rebellion by thinking we can make something good come out of it,"

"Remember, Joseph went from the pit to the prison to the palace,"

and

"I never knew the joy of my salvation until I knew the misery of my sin."

Do not be held captive to your own desires. There is freedom waiting on the other side of obedience. Let go and let God lead you.

CHAPTER 11

YEAR 2020

Romans 12:12 and Hebrews 12:12

Rejoice in hope, be patient in tribulation, be constant in prayer. Romans 12:12

Therefore, since we are surrounded by such a great cloud of witnesses, let us throw off everything that hinders and the sin that so easily entangles. And let us run with perseverance the race marked out for us, fixing our eyes on Jesus, the pioneer and perfecter of faith. For the joy set before him he endured the cross, scorning its shame, and sat down at the right hand of the throne of God. Hebrews 12:12

The Year of COVID-19—Hallelujah, Anyway!

After seeing and hearing Katherine Wolf at Passion City Church at the Women's Grove Event, I realized what I really desire is to live my best life, whatever God says that is. While reading the book Suffer Strong by Katherine and Jay Wolf, I highlighted and marked so many pages in the book. This book spoke volumes for me when I was at the point of PTSD, while struggling with where and what now.

The trauma of the last decade was over, but the effects of the trauma were just hitting me. When the song by Third Day, "Surrender," came to mind, I realized that was what God was saying to me. He was not saying don't run; He was saying to surrender it to Him.

Surrender, by Third Day

When the day began
And you opened your eyes
No, you didn't recognize
What you were seeing
Then it all came back
You remembered where you've been
Well, it never seems to end
And you're still running
Will you ever change your mind?
You're almost out of time
You better give up
Gotta stop running
It's the end of the line
It's time to surrender
Hands up

So here I was in 2020, ten years later and still doing what I had begun to do to cope with life inside the endurance race of life and addiction—I ran. I ran because I thought I should. I ran to relieve stress. I ran to hear God speak. I ran to forget what was, and I kept running until I clearly heard God say, "Stop running" and "Live your best life doing my running. I have set your race before you. Run your race I am setting out for you."

"Therefore, since we are surrounded by such a great cloud of witnesses, let us throw off everything that hinders and the sin that so easily entangles. And let us run with perseverance the race marked out for us, fixing our eyes on Jesus, the pioneer and perfecter of faith." Hebrews 12:1-2

It was time for me to stop just as quickly as Forrest Gump stopped and see where God wanted me to find my "best life." It was not about just running but running His race that He set before me.

What were the things that filled my soul in 2020? It was not training as I had thought. When asked by the trainer I had hired to get "better" if I wanted to exercise or train, I had finally recognized after a few months, the training was over; it was only the exercise that would remain for now. My time was needed for more than training. Something different would be required now, something I was not sure of but knew I needed to search and find.

I am letting go of certain responsibilities and putting in order the priorities God laid on my heart. I let go of the 2020 IRONMAN 70.3 relay I was to participate in. I let go of more work responsibilities. I let go of extra demands I allowed others to place on me knowing that in hindsight, I gave everything and everyone my time and energy except for my number one priority, God.

Hindsight is really 2020, and in 2020, I needed to work on placing God first and my husband second. When you have a husband like mine in your life, it is easy to put them at the bottom of the to-do list because they are the least trouble. He has been good to be placed wherever in my "to-do list" that I place him. He is not always happy about it, but he has accepted it and gone with whatever flow I am in. My husband has given me much grace and mercy without even recognizing it. I have also had to give him much grace and mercy over these last ten years, but the difference is he does it without thinking about it. I do it, challenging myself to follow through with it. His comes naturally; mine does not.

I am still fighting the tendency to see what "training" is needed for the day. I fight the need internally to get on a bike, run, etc., but I recognize it, pray about it, and ask God to show me where I am to be. Instead of cycling on the trainer this morning, God showed me my place was to be sitting, processing, and writing. This is the race set out for me on this day, in this month and year. What tomorrow holds, I do not know, but I will begin to run His race of life and find my best life, no matter what that looks like.

One of my dear friends and I headed out for the beach on February 18, 2020. We arrived, settled into our condo, and set up to write, study God's word through our Bible studies and find comfort and peace in our time away. On the next morning, I began my reading, writing, and back to running. I got in my head to go run six miles. I would run three miles toward Pier Park in Panama City Beach, Florida, and would turn and run the remaining three. I was having a hard time breathing, my heart rate stayed too high, and so I stopped at mile 3 and walked back on the beach.

I had to ask myself, didn't I just write a few days ago that I would stop training? I did not. I was going to see if I could run the six miles and be ready for a half-marathon in two weeks. Some things are so hard to stop when it is in your nature to be busy, and train and these habits have been formed. I had created a habit to always be training for something, which is not bad, unless God wants you to Stop, Pause, And Redirect, and if not for Him, most likely just for my well-being.

Stop and ask yourself where you are stuck? What habit or addiction has control over you.

On February 20, 2020, I began my morning with a conscience effort of what God was asking of me. I wrote my prayer so that I could stay focused on what I was praying.

Dear heavenly Father,

I do want my best life to begin now.

Lord, I cannot go back except to write about my story in hopes of helping others and finishing what I have felt You wanted me to do, which was write.

I am so wrapped up in doing what is right with work, my health, writing, being there for the ones I love, and all at the same time, I am trying to keep my heart rate and blood pressure from going haywire.

Lord, help me discern between letting go of activities and responsibilities versus a health issue. Is my HR and BP due to PTSD, trauma, or is it a health problem?

I could not run well at the beach yesterday without my heart rate jumping to over 160. Is it anxiety, stress, or something You are trying to show me that is causing this feeling?

Lord, help me this week to calm my mind, clean up my eating, and remove the things that can affect my well-being.

I want to live my best life but, Lord, I need You to show me how.

What stays, what goes, and how do I Grow?

In your name I pray and praise You.

Amen.

Then I got up, heading to the kitchen to begin my daily Bible studies, and felt Him telling me, "Don't try so hard," and then I looked outside at the ocean, the sand, and the skies and felt Him telling me, "Enjoy the blessings."

My praise song from listening while running yesterday and from today's study in Flourish saying to choose a worship song and listen to it every day for the next seven days is "Mountain of God" by Third Day.

I did not even have to work to find that. God provided it to me yesterday on my run so I would be ready to listen and hear what He wants me to hear.

Mountain of God, by Third Day

Thought that I was all alone
Broken and afraid
But You were there with me
Yes, you were there with me
And I didn't even know
That I had lost my way
But You were there with me
Yes, you were there with me

And then as if God had been preparing me in 2020 to slow down, get life in order, remove some of the tasks and duties I felt obligated to accomplish, we were overtaken by the COVID-19 virus that swept across the world and is now hitting the United States of America extremely hard. And I had plenty of time to write!

My husband and I have been discussing many times over the last couple of years how we are ready for less obligations and to see what slowing down looks like. That time never came because we continually filled our days with what we thought was important until all we thought was important was taken away.

When work, events, and activities were taken away, and all we must do is stay, "shelter in place" for what might be a couple of weeks to months, has shown us what is important. I wrote this week in a blog that I share, "Are You Essential?" This seems to be the biggest statement right now for individuals and businesses to continue being out in full force. I think it is a question we all need to ask ourselves now and always. Are we essential, and if not, we had better find out how we can be essential? Anything less would be a waste for us and others.

Article written on April 1, 2020:

Who and What Is Essential?

Who would have thought just a couple of months ago that we would all have to ask ourselves these questions?

Is my business essential?
Am I essential to my business?
Is that position and job essential?
Who is at risk?
Who is to take a risk?

Who claims we are essential, and are we essential?

Definition of essential: necessary; extremely important.

In my 2019 goal and task setting for the 2020 year, I did not ask these questions and did not know that I should. I am goal oriented, not only in my business life but in my personal life as well.

I had a full calendar of events, to-dos, meetings, and goals I planned on accomplishing and completing in the first quarter of this year. I had a full calendar of events, especially in April to see all these goals come to completion. The year 2020 has not turned out like any of us had planned. Quite the contrary, we have had to reassess our goals and just put them aside in business and personally. Then our new goal was to figure out how to isolate ourselves from family, friends, and coworkers all at once.

So, where we started this year with all these new year resolutions and goals for business and personal have now turned into a bigger, deeper, and probably more important question and goal to recognize; that is, am I essential and in what have I been called to do the essential?

First, is my business essential?

The Georgia Association of Realtors, the National Association of Realtors and our local Carpet Capital Association of Realtors are all working hard to keep us and the public informed during this critical time. We believe we are an essential business because homeownership is a huge component to economic impact locally, statewide, and nationwide. There are people that for whatever reason, still need to buy or sell homes during this time. Job transfers, deaths, marriages, loss of jobs, and financial burdens require people to move, whether buying or selling during this time.

Real estate is a market that, during good times or bad times, is always essential. And where it is an essential business, we can do it with more social distancing than many other businesses. We can do remote meetings, video-remote closings and e-signatures, virtual showings, and virtual listing appointments. Our local, state, and national boards have been working around the clock to keep our business essential and functioning to continue to fulfill the needs within this industry, and we are doing everything in our power to be an essential player in our communities and families during this time. We are staying in tune with all information from our board associations along with the state of Georgia and national broadcast.

This is an unprecedented time, but we will get to the other side of it, and we will learn more in these months about our businesses and ourselves than we have in many years.

I think the biggest impact we will take from this is finding out if we are essential, and if so, how do we use our skills to benefit others, and more importantly, are we as individuals essential, and if not, what do we need to change about ourselves so that we are essential.

If we do not have something to give others that makes us essential, then we are missing the boat. We were not put here on this earth to be unessential, but essential, so now is the time to find out what makes you essential.

And last, but not least, what do we do personally that is essential, and what is wasted time?

During these few weeks, all the busyness of everyday life has slowed down. I am not planning a bike ride, having weekly meetings, training for an upcoming race, traveling, working as much, taking care of everyday tasks as I was before. This is the time for all of us to see what is important and essential and let go of some of the nonessentials that have been creating stress and unnecessary busyness and taking away from the essentials that are important for ourselves and for those we serve.

I hope that when we get through this, our country will be a better place working together as one, not divided, that our businesses and our communities support and love each other better and that I fully recognize my place in all of it and where I am as the most essential individual in whatever my calling turns out to be!

Stay healthy, safe and Go, Be Essential! Be Essential!

Additional questions and scriptures:

Do you want to be Healed? Do you want to be Saved?

There is a Way, and the Way will set you Free.

If you declare with your mouth, "Jesus is Lord," and believe in your heart that God raised him from the dead, you will be saved. For it is with your heart that you believe and are justified, and it is with your mouth that you profess your faith and are saved. Romans 10:9

As Scripture says, "Anyone who believes in him will never be put to shame." For there is no difference between Jew and Gentile—the same Lord is Lord of all and richly blesses all who call on him, for, "Everyone who calls on the name of the Lord will be saved." Romans 10:9-12 NIV

Consequently, faith comes from hearing the message, and the message is heard through the word about Christ. Romans 10:17 NIV

Grace and peace to you from God our Father and the Lord Jesus Christ. Praise be to the God and Father of our Lord Jesus Christ, the Father of compassion and the God of all comfort, who comforts us in all our troubles, so that we can comfort those in any trouble with the comfort we ourselves receive from God. 2 Corinthians 1:2–4

On February 22, 2020, I rose earlier than in the previous mornings while at the beach and began my Flourish Bible study, Week 6, Day 5, pulling this week's study into completion.

This week was in Psalm 119:145–176. What I had written throughout this week's study was about rising before dawn, crying for help, putting my hope in His word, eyes staying open, meditating, learning, not forgetting, and looking for His precepts.

At all times, I need to call, look, rise, learn, meditate, hear, not forget, and look to God! And as my friend said, with adversity, stay focused and mindful, stay present and mindful of the moment. This is what I am trying to do.

While reflecting on these scriptures, something kept me questioning just what it meant by salvation.

How did the psalmist define salvation as he continued to write about it in these scriptures? The psalmist was a believer, so why did he long for God's salvation and wait for the Lord's salvation? What did this mean and what did it mean for me?

Per Wikipedia, salvation is Christianity or deliverance or redemption; it is the saving of human beings from death and separation from God "by Christ's death and resurrection."

Another definition says it is the saving of our soul from sin and its consequences, deliverance, redemption which equals grace.

Born again means everything they have been taught as Christians becomes real, and they develop a direct and personal relationship with God. And this is what hit me as soon as I was defining salvation which took me to born again.

Up to 2010, I had been taught about faith in Christ, I had been raised in the teachings of the Bible, but I wasn't "born again" until I had started crying out to God for help, for my family and for my son's safety. I needed salvation for me to be delivered and redeemed as well as for our son to be delivered and redeemed.

I recognized that I could not live with any separation from God but only with His presence. Salvation is not only something that will happen in the eternal, later after death, but is deliverance and redemption in the here and now so that we see the eternal life and place our hope in His salvation.

Blessed be the God and Father of our Lord Jesus Christ, the Father of mercies and God of all comfort, who comforts us in all our afflictions, so that we may be able to comfort those who are in any affliction, with the comfort with which we ourselves are comforted by God. 2 Corinthians 1:3–4

Psalm 4:8 is my verse of the day on February 22, 2020.

In peace I will lie down and sleep, for you alone, Lord, make me dwell in safety. Psalm 4:8 Amen.

One of my desires and goal became to be a Propel Women. I read The Propel Woman and instantly knew that is what I wanted.

I want to be a Propel Woman!

Find more about the Propel Woman on https://www.propelwomen.org/

At the ending of this writing, I received two messages, one saying that the Lord had guided this person to send me this song, "God of All My Days" by Casting Crowns, and the other was to listen to this new podcast by Sarah Jones, "What Did Jesus Say," from Mark 1:14–15.

I encourage you to find the song and listen to it too.

God of All My Days, by Casting Crowns

And read,

A Ministry of Hope podcast by Sarah Jones http://sarahdecosimojones. blogspot.com/

Sarah Jones has been a blessing during these years, not only because of her teaching but also her love, dedication, and prayers always. Sarah Jones is essential; just ask anyone that knows her! Thanks for setting such a great example of the love of Christ to all you know and reach in your ministry.

I pray to be a propel and an essential woman for those that need me and those that the Lord leads me to, whether in home, work, or in areas of need.

While I turn over into this next decade that is beginning in isolation for all of us, I will pray, love, and share what God calls me to, if only through a website!

https://lisaheyer.com/ Endurance Race of Life Race for your life!
www.LisaHeyer.com

This is my story, not our sons or anyone else. This is the story of me, a mother, frightened, heartbroken, dealing with my child in the dark depths of addiction. When it gets hard, and it will, know whose you are. Dig deep into the only one that can comfort you to the degree you need to be comforted and lean hard because there will be times that are easier and times that are harder but keep your faith and remember God has you and your loved ones. Your loved one is God's too.

We all have different battles and strongholds, but the answer is always the same. We need God because He can do more with us and them than you will ever be able to do. There isn't a quick fix, but there is hope in the One that can heal.

Addiction has no boundaries, not social, economic, geographical limits, or any other limits when it finds its home. It is not selective of race, religion, age; however, the younger it gets you, the harder it is to overcome. It is important for me to express how anyone, any family, and anyone's son or daughter could be where our son found himself. Addiction doesn't stay in one arena. It will meet you wherever you are so beware; the devil comes to kill, steal, and destroy.

But God!

I hope to start and finish my life's race with these two verses.

What about you?

Therefore, since we are surrounded by such a great cloud of witnesses, let us throw off everything that hinders and the sin that so easily entangles. And let us run with perseverance the race marked out for us, fixing our eyes on Jesus, the pioneer and perfecter of faith. For the joy set before him he endured the cross, scorning its shame, and sat down at the right hand of the throne of God. Consider him who endured such opposition from sinners, so that you will not grow weary and lose heart. Hebrews 12:1–3

For I am already being poured out like a drink offering, and the time for my departure is near. I have fought the good fight, I have finished the race, I have kept the faith. Now there is in store for me the crown of righteousness, which the Lord, the righteous Judge, will award to me on that day—and not only to me, but also to all who have longed for his appearing. 2 Timothy 4:6–8

ABOUT THE AUTHOR

Lisa is a wife, mother, grandmother, daughter, sister, and owner/ broker of Better Homes and Gardens Jackson Realty, soon entering the retirement years of life. These are the roles she plays, but mostly, she is a child of God and a woman of faith that has grown tremendously through her endurance race of life and her son's endurance race of addiction as she wrote about in her first book, Endurance Race of Life and Addiction—Race for Your Life.

She was raised in a church by wonderful Christian parents, attending church services every Sunday morning and evening and on Wednesday nights as well. As an adult, she attended years of women's Bible studies and continued the weekly Sunday and Wednesday services and studies. She was known by one of her friends as the church lady, which she was, but she found out later that being a "church lady" meant she believed in God, but she didn't know what all that entailed. Her real faith came when she would lose her fifteen-year-old son to addiction for the next eight-plus years. That was having faith without seeing, and only then, did she learn who God is and what He can do in and for her.

God is the Savior that she had studied about growing up, but she finally had the opportunity to experience Him in reality, not just in Bible studies. God has carried her through so much, and His love, mercy, and grace never failed. She just needed to learn how to surrender, trust, and run the race set before her.

As it says in Hebrews 12:1–2, "Therefore, since we are surrounded by such a great cloud of witnesses, let us throw off everything that hinders and the sin that so easily entangles. And let us run with perseverance the race marked out for us, fixing our eyes on Jesus, the pioneer and perfecter of faith."

MY STORIES, HIS TIMING, AND THE SCATTERNESS AND HALLELUJAHS

Thanksgiving to the Lord for His Great Works of Deliverance

Psalm 107: 1-2 NIV

1 Give thanks to the Lord, for he is good.
his love endures forever.

2 Let the redeemed of the Lord tell their story.

Printed in the United States
by Baker & Taylor Publisher Services